# The Power of Choice
# A Teen's Guide to
# Finding PERSONAL
# SUCCESS

**CLAUDE B. LARSON**

Copyright © 2021 by Claude B. Larson

The Power of Choice A Teen's Guide to Finding Personal Success

All rights reserved. No part of this publication may be reproduced, distributed or transmitted in any form or by any means, including photocopying, recording, or other electronic or mechanical methods, without the prior written permission of the publisher, except in the case of brief quotations embodied in critical reviews and certain other noncommercial uses permitted by copyright law.

Although the author and publisher have made every effort to ensure that the information in this book was correct at press time, the author and publisher do not assume and hereby disclaim any liability to any party for any loss, damage, or disruption caused by errors or omissions, whether such errors or omissions result from negligence, accident, or any other cause.

Adherence to all applicable laws and regulations, including international, federal, state and local governing professional licensing, business practices, advertising, and all other aspects of doing business in the US, Canada or any other jurisdiction is the sole responsibility of the reader and consumer.

Neither the author nor the publisher assumes any responsibility or liability whatsoever on behalf of the consumer or reader of this material. Any perceived slight of any individual or organization is purely unintentional.

The resources in this book are provided for informational purposes only and should not be used to replace the specialized training and professional judgment of a health care or mental health care professional.

Neither the author nor the publisher can be held responsible for the use of the information provided within this book. Please always consult a trained professional before making any decision regarding treatment of yourself or others.

ISBN: 978-1-7357258-0-2 print version
978-1-7357258-1-9 ebook version

Cover design by 100Covers
Interior design by FormattedBooks

This book is dedicated to my students. Without you this book would have never come into being. Thank you for making my journey a more inspiring and worthwhile adventure.

For additional exercises and extensions of each chapter in printable format.

Life is a matter of choices, and every choice you make makes you."

—*John C. Maxwell*

# Contents

Foreword ................................................................................................................. vii

| | | |
|---|---|---|
| Chapter 1 | Your Dirty Mind ................................................................................ 1 |
| Chapter 2 | How's Life Treating You? ................................................................... 3 |
| Chapter 3 | What Are You Willing To Do? ............................................................ 7 |
| Chapter 4 | 10,000 Hours .................................................................................... 11 |
| Chapter 5 | All You Need is Love ....................................................................... 15 |
| Chapter 6 | How Do You Want to Suffer? .......................................................... 19 |
| Chapter 7 | What is the Worst Punishment in the World? ................................. 23 |
| Chapter 8 | Walk the Plank ................................................................................ 27 |
| Chapter 9 | How You Do Anything is How You Do Everything ........................ 29 |
| Chapter 10 | What's Your Problem? ..................................................................... 33 |
| Chapter 11 | I Like Me, I Like Me Not ................................................................. 37 |
| Chapter 12 | Have You Ever Felt Unappreciated? ................................................ 41 |
| Chapter 13 | You Snooze, You Lose ..................................................................... 45 |
| Chapter 14 | The Domino Effect .......................................................................... 49 |
| Chapter 15 | Guilty or Innocent ........................................................................... 53 |
| Chapter 16 | Grow Yourself, Grow Your Happiness ............................................. 57 |
| Chapter 17 | Living Large .................................................................................... 63 |
| Chapter 18 | What Is the Highest Function of Your Mind? ................................. 65 |
| Chapter 19 | Who Would You Bet On? ................................................................ 69 |
| Chapter 20 | Deliberate Time ............................................................................... 73 |
| Chapter 21 | Beware of Vampires! ........................................................................ 77 |
| Chapter 22 | It's Not What You Look at That Matters, It's What You See ........... 81 |
| Chapter 23 | Imagination is Everything ............................................................... 85 |
| Chapter 24 | Get Out of Control .......................................................................... 89 |
| Chapter 25 | What if All of Your Misfortunes Were Your Fortunes? .................... 93 |
| Chapter 26 | A Story of Two Monks ..................................................................... 97 |
| Chapter 27 | Creating a Good Day ..................................................................... 101 |
| Chapter 28 | Life is 10 Percent What Happens to You and 90 Percent How You React to It ............. 105 |
| Chapter 29 | The Key to Success ........................................................................ 109 |
| Chapter 30 | Get Your Hands Dirty ................................................................... 113 |

# Foreword

Let me begin by thanking you for picking up this book. It is a compilation of lessons that are designed to help you make choices about your life and how you want it to look right now and in the future. There are so many things competing for your attention in this fast-paced world. As a teen, you are also faced with so much pressure to fit in with the crowd. What's cool changes every day and the daily demand to keep up can be exhausting. Add to this, the burden that you have to figure out what you should be keeping up with and life really becomes a challenge.

As a middle school science teacher, I have spent most of my 25 years in education teaching young adults. It has been both rewarding and frustrating to watch my students learn the difficult lessons that help them develop into amazing people. These students and my experiences with them have provided the inspiration for this book. My intention is to help you navigate these years of early adulthood in a way that allows you to set some goals for your future and create a plan for how to achieve them.

In this constantly changing world that we live in, we all experience confusion about what you should be paying attention to. Many important life habits get pushed aside. This book is a beginning. It is a place to write down your ideas and really think about how you want your life to turn out. The chapters and activities are designed to give you time to think about things in a way that perhaps you haven't done so before. Ultimately, the goal is to help you decide what kind of person you want to be and help you figure out how to get there.

The chapters aren't about any of the latest trends. In fact, these ideas are old school and timeless. How you apply them to your life will be as unique as you are. I hope you find the contents of this book useful as well as entertaining. More importantly, I hope that what you learn about yourself allows you grow more rewarding relationships and habits. Ultimately, the choices that only *you* can make have the power to direct your life's course. Let's begin!

# Your Dirty Mind

I want to let you in on a little secret. For thousands of years, the greatest achievers and thinkers were in touch with this secret. Because it is timeless, it is as true today as it was so many years ago. It works for anybody who uses it and for any purpose. In recent time, this secret has been buried under layers of distractions such as television, social media, video games, and the fast-paced trend of the day lifestyle we live in. The only way to use this secret to your advantage is to know it and apply it to your life. Knowing it is not enough. You have to do something with it.

Here it is: What you think about, you become. It is as simple as it is powerful. The power of your thoughts creates the person that you will become. Once you understand this idea, you become very careful of what you think about. If you repeatedly fill your head with gossip, worrying, complaining, rumors, and drama, your mind will be filled with things that attract problems and negative thought patterns to you. If you create thoughts of thankfulness for what you do have, instead of what is lacking, you grow gratitude. If you focus on positive ideas about the people and circumstances around you, you will have positive feelings toward those people and events, and positive things will be attracted to you. This powerful secret works for the here and now as well as for the future.

Consider that your mind is very much like a pile of dirt. The mind will allow anything that you plant there to grow. You can sow seeds of negativity and grow feelings of resentment and anger. Or you can plant seeds of gratitude and positive thinking and increase feelings of happiness and joy in your life. Remember, your mind is like soil. What you plant in your mind will grow because the mind will water and care for those thoughts without discrimination. Once your thoughts begin to take root in your mind, they will look for other ideas that help them grow stronger and faster. If you continue to have thoughts about something you want in your life, your ideas will connect with people who want those things too. It sounds crazy, but it's true. Your thoughts will find people who have similar ideas. It's not a coincidence, it's an energetic connection. When your thought wants to grow bigger and stronger it connects to another thought that helps it expand.

Make a list of some things in your life right now that you feel positive about.

_____

_____

_____

_____

How much time do you spend thinking about them?

_____

_____

_____

This is a little harder. Make a list of things that you wish were happening in your life.

_____

_____

_____

_____

_____

What would you have to change about your thoughts to help these things expand in your life?

_____

_____

_____

_____

_____

# How's Life Treating You?

Take a moment and write down the answers to the following questions.

- How's life treating you?
- How's school treating you?
- How's your family treating you?
- How are your friends treating you?
- How are your extracurricular activities (sports, band, chorus, dance, special classes or lessons) treating you?

Do you have the same answer for each of these questions?

_____

Why do you think this is so?

_____

_____

More than anything else, your attitude determines the quality of your life. It is the one thing that you can change to affect the rest of your life. Start with one simple question. How is life treating me? If you say it is treating you well, then you have a positive attitude about life. If you say it is treating you lousy, then you have a negative attitude about life. It's that simple. You can substitute any of the questions above to check your attitude about these aspects of your life. Chances are that if you think someone or something is treating you poorly then you have a negative attitude about that person or thing.

**Finding Personal Success**

Your attitude creates your reality. The way you view the world is often a reflection of how you view yourself. Carrying around negative thoughts or attitudes can cause you to have a negative opinion of yourself. Similarly, focusing on positive thoughts and having an optimistic attitude can boost your self-worth. You have the power to change how you see yourself and the world simply by changing your attitude.

Here's a little story about a farmer from long ago.

A farmer sits on the side of a dirt road looking out at his field of crops. Along the road comes a covered wagon with a family that is looking to settle and build a house in the nearby town. The family stops and asks the farmer "We're looking to build a house and live in that town up ahead. What kind of people will we find there?" The farmer says to the wagon driver "What were the people like where you came from?" The settlers reply, "They were nasty, lazy, mean and downright awful people. We're glad to be rid of them." The farmer says, "Well, you'll find the same kind of people in that town." After a while another covered wagon comes along with a family looking to move into the town down that road. The wagon driver asks the farmer, "We're looking to build a house and live in that town up ahead. What kind of people will we find there?" The farmer says to the wagon driver "What were the people like where you came from?" The driver says, "Where we came from the people were kind, generous, hard-working and the nicest people we ever knew." And the farmer says, "Well, you'll find the same kind of people in that town."

What you seek, you shall find. If you are looking for people who will sit with you and complain, gossip, and speak negative thoughts, you will surely find them. If you choose to look for people who are kind, generous and have a positive attitude, you'll find them too. Your attitude is one thing that is completely within your control. Remember from the previous chapter that whatever you plant in your mind will grow there. The decision you have left is what kind of attitude you want to have? Shifting your thoughts to something that creates a more positive attitude brings a more optimistic reality.

Write down two areas of your life where your experiences could benefit from a change of attitude.

_____

_____

_____

_____

_____

_____

_____

_____

What could you tell yourself that would improve your attitude about those things?

_____

_____

_____

_____

_____

_____

_____

Write these messages to yourself on a couple of sticky notes and put them on your mirror, nightstand, planner, home screen, or any place that you see throughout the day. A reminder of how you want to change your attitude and what that shift will do to improve your life can be a simple yet powerful tool.

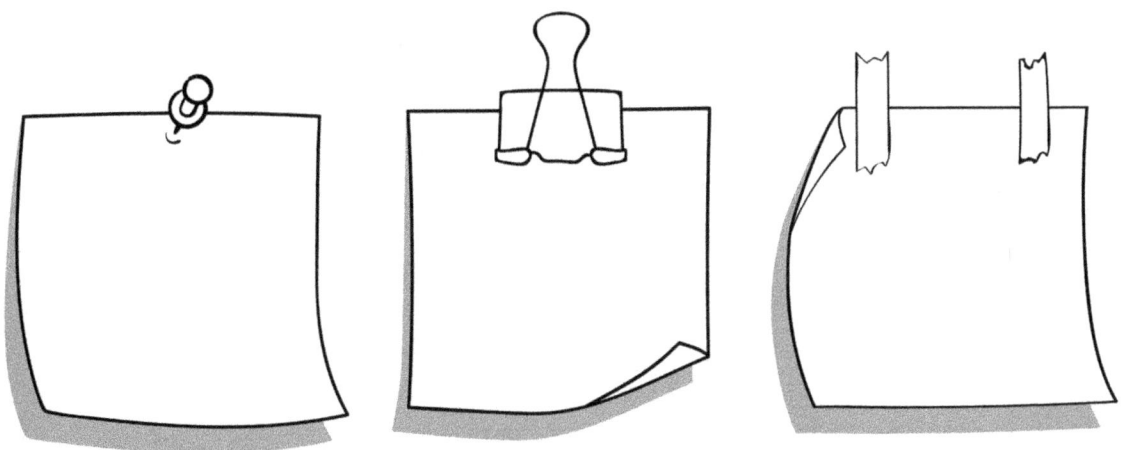

**Finding Personal Success**

# CHAPTER 3

# What Are You Willing To Do?

Take a moment to consider all the things you do in a day. Home, school, sports, activities, recreation, homework, etc. Now think about *how* you do these things. Do you put equal amount of effort into each of these areas? How do things turn out when you put in your best and most outstanding effort? Now think about the areas where you are not putting in an excellent effort. What is the outcome of the things where you put in less than your best? How does your attitude about each of these areas affect the amount of effort you are putting into the tasks you perform? Much like your attitude, you have control of how much effort you put into any task, relationship or activity. Often your effort makes the difference between an excellent outcome or a mediocre one.

Let's discuss excellence. You recognize excellence when you see it. Every professional athlete, musician, performer, and person at the top of their field has achieved excellence. How did they do it? Now let's think about our original question. What are you willing to do? For example, let's say you are on a team. You arrive at practice on time. You have your equipment. You practice and do everything the coach says and what all the other kids are doing. Great. Hopefully, you are having some fun at this. Now many kids will think that this is how the pros got to where they are. Doing everything that everyone else does. Ummm. Incorrect. If you do what everyone else does, then you will rise to the same level of everyone else. This is called average. It is also called conformity.

Conformity is the opposite of excellence. Excellence requires you to do *more* than everyone else is doing. You want to be first chair in the symphony, practice longer and more challenging music than everybody else does. You want to be a professional athlete? Watch the pros, do what they do. Practice longer and harder than everyone else on your team. Practice on your own and watch your skills excel. You want to be an artist, writer, singer, dancer, doctor, scientist or whatever… learn everything you can about it and work at it harder than everybody else. The excellent people of the world did not get there by doing what everybody else was doing. They did more until they became excellent.

Why are so many people average? Simple. They aren't willing to do the extra work. Why? Because it's work. If you are willing to work harder than everyone else at what you love, it won't necessarily be easy but once you become excellent; it will be worth it.

Write down one area of your life where you would like to put in a better effort?

_____
_____
_____
_____
_____
_____
_____
_____

What would you have to do to make that extra effort possible?

_____
_____
_____
_____
_____
_____
_____
_____

Would a shift in attitude help you achieve what you want or would you have to do something else as well?

___

How would a better effort in this area change your life?

___

# Chapter 4

# 10,000 Hours

In the last chapter you gave some thought to what it takes to become excellent at something. Basically, it takes work. However, if you are working at something that you love to do, it doesn't always feel like work. But the bad news is, sometimes it feels *exactly* like hard work. You have to keep at it even when the progress is slow.

Many people have estimated that in order to become excellent at something, I mean really world-class, it takes about 10,000 hours of deliberate practice. Let's do a little math here. So, if you decide you want to be excellent at something you need to practice it – deliberately. That means giving it your full attention: not checking your social media; watching TV while your practicing something else; not allowing interruptions and distractions to stop you from practicing. If you could commit to working at this particular thing, sport, dance, music, writing, art, public speaking, whatever, every day for 1 hour, it would take you about 27 years to be excellent at it. Hmmm. If you start right now you can reach this by the time you're about 40 years old. That seems pretty far away. What about if you practice it for 3 hours a day, every day? That would take you a little over 9 years to become excellent. That would make you about 22 years old. Now that seems a little more reasonable.

Here's the big question. Is there anything that you love so much that you would do it every day for 3 hours or more? Without allowing anyone or anything to distract you? Without getting bored with it? Something that you value more than anything else? That you could get paid to do? (After all, if you're going to be world-class, you probably want to make a living out of it.)

Here's some things that you can do, if you decide to go on a 10,000-hour journey. If a couple thousand hours into the journey you decide to change course because your deliberate practice leads you to something you like better – great! Then you've already practiced the stuff that will help you achieve excellence.

1. Learn by reading or listening to others who know how to do it and then practice like an expert.
2. Practice some more. Realize that at the beginning of this practicing you will stink at this. You could stink at this for several months or longer but, if you don't give up, you'll get better. (The payoff!)
3. Practice some more. In a few years you'll be good. Don't get too comfortable at being good if you want to be great. Once you're good, challenge yourself by learning more ways to do this thing you love. Which sometimes means that you have to go back to being lousy at it until you get better.
4. Let go of the frustration of making mistakes or going back to stinking at it while you challenge yourself. If you can't get over making mistakes, you'll never be great. Ask anybody who is world-class. Keep practicing. You are only as good as your last success. Wrote an amazing song – make the next one better. Played an amazing game – up it for the next game. Mastered a dance move or musical piece – move to a harder one. Wrote a great story – everyone will expect your next one to be better, don't disappoint them (or yourself). You get the idea.

What areas of your life do you spend your time doing something you love?

_____
_____
_____
_____
_____
_____

How has spending this time on this activity improved your skills?

_____
_____
_____
_____
_____
_____

Is it possible that this time that you have spent learning or working at something could be something you pursue as a career or life path? Where can you see the value for society in it?

_____

_____

_____

_____

_____

_____

_____

_____

_____

_____

Make a list of things that you could do that would help you become excellent at this particular interest.

| _____ | _____ |
| _____ | _____ |
| _____ | _____ |
| _____ | _____ |
| _____ | _____ |
| _____ | _____ |
| _____ | _____ |

# All You Need is Love

Take a few moments to make a list of everything you love.

_____  _____
_____  _____
_____  _____
_____  _____
_____  _____
_____  _____
_____  _____
_____  _____
_____  _____
_____  _____

Now that you have made a list of what you love, examine it and notice how far down you got before you wrote yourself. Did you write yourself on your list? Perhaps you overlooked it.

So, let's assume that you either wrote yourself on your list or you meant to write yourself on your list. Either way, you should be on the list of things you love. Right? We all know someone who loves themselves — at least when they look in the mirror — it's considered being conceited. That's not what we're talking about here. Loving yourself means that you want what is best for you. You want good things for your life. You value yourself and your life. After all, if you have written down a person or people on your list of things you love, you surely want what's best for them. So, if you want what's best for you, that's healthy thinking.

Self-love. If you love yourself, how would you treat yourself? Would you say negative things to yourself in your head? Probably not. If you love yourself, how would you behave? Smoke? Drink alcohol? Take drugs? Let people use you? Eat unhealthy food? Let your body get weak so it doesn't serve you? Probably not. Yet, we see people do this all the time. Perhaps they love themselves, but have gotten on the wrong path to showing themselves some kindness. Once you sit down and think about how you want your life to be — because you love yourself — it makes it clearer what choices are in your best interest. What behaviors do you engage in and not engage in? What people do you surround yourself with and what people do you avoid? If you allow loving yourself to be what guides you in these choices, the decisions become much clearer (but not necessarily easier).

What would you do to make every one of your days the very best? Are you doing that? This forces you to make some choices that might be challenging. Maybe you need to choose the thing that no one else is doing. Choose the thing that is in your best interest.

Let's expand your mind from not only thinking about yourself but to thinking about others. Do you think that you deserve to be loved not only by yourself but by others? Do you think everyone deserves to be loved, if not by you, by someone? Do you treat everyone with this belief in mind? What needs to change for you to treat everyone like they deserve to be loved? Because once you love yourself, you can see that everyone should love themselves. If you want what is best for you, then everyone wants what is best for them. So, if you believe that you deserve to be loved, and everyone else deserves to be loved, it affects how you treat people. Take a moment and consider how you treat people. Even if you are not friends or family with a particular person, would you agree that they should have someone in their life who loves them and who they can express their love to?

Choose one person you care about and write down all the ways you show them you love them.

_____

_____

_____

_____

Now, choose someone with whom you are not friends with – perhaps someone who you consider difficult to get along with. Remember that everyone deserves to be loved by someone. How do you treat them?

_____
_____
_____
_____
_____

What thoughts could you change to help you remember that they are loved by someone?

_____
_____
_____
_____
_____

How do you think these changes would affect that person?

_____
_____
_____
_____

Finally, if you treated everyone with more kindness how would it change you?

_____
_____
_____
_____
_____

# Chapter 6

# How Do You Want to Suffer?

In the previous chapter, we took a look at love and self-love. I think we'd all agree that we want to have a life full of good things and that we want to have people in our lives that we love and that love us. So, the question "How do you want to suffer?" might not be the first thing that comes to mind when you think about loving yourself. Consider this, if you want something you will give yourself a reason to go get it – that's motivation. Your reason will cause you to seek your reward.

So, what do you want? If you want to be smart, you'll read, study, learn, and do things that grow your brain. Do you want to be strong? Then you will do things that make your body stronger – exercise, eat healthy, and actually do things that make you stronger. You want to be happier? (Who doesn't?) Then you will make choices that make you feel good about yourself – things that grow your self-respect. If you want to be kind, you'll find opportunities to express kindness and you'll look for other kind people to connect with.

Here's the challenge. Doing schoolwork or studying is hard. So is exercise or making healthy food choices. Giving up your time to do kind acts for others can also have its challenges. You'd rather play video games, go outside and play with your friends, text, or watch TV. You'd rather eat the pizza and French fries and ice cream. You would rather do the things that are easy and bring immediate pleasure.

Here's how it works. You need to suffer. The title of the chapter is not "Do You Want to Suffer?" It's "*How Do You Want to Suffer?*" Want to be smart? Do your classwork, your homework, study and read. What happens next, you say? Well, you get good grades, you know stuff and understand things. Your self-esteem increases, you like yourself better. Maybe your parents notice your grades and life gets better at home. It takes self-discipline. Doing it without being told by someone else. Want to be strong and healthy? Make the choices that bring you that reward. Want to be a better musician? Writer? Artist? Whatever? It requires you to tell yourself to do it and then… actually do it! This process might last a pretty long time. Remember that to be first-rate at things you might have to work at it for 10,000 hours – many of those hours will be difficult. Eventually those hours are the actually the reward for the time you put in and the times you stuck with it when the going was tough. Here's the suffering.

Because you have the choice of how you want to suffer, there's also a second option. Don't apply your self-discipline. Don't tell yourself to do things that will lead you to improving whatever it is in your life that you want to improve. No homework. No studying. Poor grades. No exercise. Weak body. No practice. No improvement. Maybe you sit the bench, if you make the team at all. Maybe you don't get picked for the special group in band, art, math, or whatever. How do you feel about yourself? Maybe not so good. That's regret. You missed the opportunity to do the things you could have done and now that the time is gone, you're left with only the regret that you didn't make the effort. Here's the suffering.

Either way, there's some suffering. How you want to suffer is a choice but, the actual suffering is not optional. Self-discipline – you suffer to get where you want to go. Regret – you suffer, get nowhere and that time has passed.

Think about your life as it is right now. Write down one or two things that you would like to improve in your life. This could be anything from a relationship that you have with a family member or friend to something you want to create, achieve or experience. Being aware of what you want to improve is an important first step.

_____

_____

_____

_____

Take each item that you wrote and make a list of things that you can actually do that would help move you in the direction you want to go. Make sure these are things that are within your control. You cannot change anyone else's behavior. You can only change what you say or do in any situation.

_____

_____

_____

_____

_____

_____

_____

_____

_____

_____

_____

_____

Circle the top three things that you can do that would help you get to where you want to go.

Write down a plan of what you can do to get to where you want to go. Feel free to enlist the help of others to be your cheerleaders, supporters, or people who will hold you accountable for doing what you said you would. Include simple and more complex actions. Break it down into the smallest steps possible. Now, decide what you will do first and move forward with your plan.

_____

_____

_____

_____

_____

_____

_____

# What is the Worst Punishment in the World?

Laughter. Yup. That is correct. Laughter is the worst punishment in the world. People will do almost anything to avoid being the target of people's laughter. We have all had the experience of being laughed at. When you tripped and spilled your lunch, dropped your books, or made that less than graceful landing in Phys. Ed class. Maybe you wore something to school that you thought was pretty cool and someone made fun of you. Not such a good feeling.

Laughter is such a terrible punishment that there is a tribe in the far northern region of North America that uses laughter as the punishment for stealing. If a tribe member steals, everyone in the tribe points at them and laughs wherever they go. Public humiliation. It seems like a simple thing, but how it makes a person feel will probably change their mind about ever stealing anything again.

We all like to feel accepted. Consider what you have done to avoid being laughed at. Perhaps you've worn or not worn something? That's an easy one. After all, you want to fit in with everybody else so dressing similarly to the group is a good way to avoid being made fun of. You can give yourself a break on this. Have you purchased or not purchased something because you thought one of your friends would make fun of you? Have you been confused and not raised your hand to ask a question in class? Joined or not joined a sport, club, or group to avoid being laughed at? The fact that you base decisions on whether or not people will laugh at you speaks to how strong the punishment of laughter actually is.

Think about something that you want to do or have that might cause your friends or family laugh at you. Do you still want it? If the answer is yes, then maybe it's worth having or doing despite what others think. What is it that you love so much that you would be willing to be laughed at to do it? How would it feel to pursue that idea or dream and ignore the people laughing at you?

**Finding Personal Success**

Now, imagine that someone else wants something else that you don't see the point in having or doing. What would you say? What does that say about you if you laugh at them?

Take a moment and think about a time that you laughed at or made fun of someone for something they wore or did. Reverse the focus for a moment. Instead of thinking about how that person felt, which was probably pretty crummy, think about what this says about you as a person. Making fun of someone else is not the act of a very kindhearted person. It probably also takes you out of the competition to be a supporter or cheerleader for whatever that person wants to achieve.

Write down anything that you want so badly that you would risk being laughed at by others.

_____

_____

_____

_____

If you achieved this or became this, how would the opinion of others affect you?

_____

_____

_____

_____

Think of a time that you made fun of or laughed at another person.

_____

_____

_____

_____

Think of some kinder responses you could have if someone does something around you that you think is foolish or not worthy of your time.

_____

_____

_____

_____

How would that change your relationship with this person?

_____

_____

_____

_____

How would it change how you feel about yourself as a person?

_____

_____

_____

_____

# CHAPTER 8

## Walk the Plank

If there was a plank of wood on the floor that was twelve inches wide, four inches thick, and twelve feet long, everyone could walk from one end to the other. However, if that same plank is suspended between two buildings 100 feet above the ground, suddenly our confidence about walking across that plank is a little shaky. If you can do something at your house or in a small group, why is it so intimidating to do in front of a large audience? We've all seen the star athlete miss a free throw, drop the pass, or choke at the key moment of the game. They've made a million free throws, catches, and great moves in practice. But when the stands are full and all eyes are on them – different story. What's the difference? Courage.

Courage is a muscle. Like any other muscle, you don't start lifting using 200-pound weights. Maybe you start with a five-pound weight and you work your way up. What does this look like? Maybe you introduce yourself to someone new, join a new club or sport, try something you've never done before, try a new food, stand up for yourself when someone is being mean. Small acts of courage build your confidence until you are able to do larger acts of courage. If you start small and keep doing larger and larger acts of courage, then you will become a courageous person.

There's a phenomenon that I have observed about 2 percent of people. Ninety-eight percent of people want to feel secure. They want to have a secure job, know what is going to happen before it happens, and avoid situations where they can't anticipate the outcome. You know them. They will only go to the party if they know exactly who's going to be there. They prefer ordering the same meal at a restaurant because they know what they're going to get. They haven't really been using their courage muscle. The other 2 percent of people take risks. They are willing to step into the unknown, fail, get up, and try again. They think differently and take opportunities. They also make opportunities for themselves. They do things like meet new people, stretch themselves to see what they are capable of and take a chance at something not knowing what to expect. These people have courage. They also are not afraid of failure so they are willing to take the risk. The pay-off? They get the greater reward. Looking back at Chapter 3 about excellence, you will recall that you can only get better if you are willing to make mistakes and learn from them.

There's an old saying, "You can't get to second base keeping your foot on first." You might get tagged out, but you might also slide in and be safe. Taking the risk is a way to get ahead, and it can be pretty exciting. What act of courage are you willing to attempt to get the reward of confidence? Start small – or jump in and start big. What happens may surprise you.

What are some things you would like to do but just keep making excuses about? Usually these excuses are based on fear of failure.

_____

_____

_____

_____

_____

Look at each thing on your list. What would it feel like to do that thing? What would be the best possible outcome?

_____

_____

_____

_____

_____

_____

_____

Remember that taking a chance grows your courage, no matter how things turn out.

# CHAPTER 9

# How You Do Anything is How You Do Everything

Consider this thought: How you do anything is how you do everything. If you break it down, it means that no matter what task you are doing, big or small, you do it with the same level of effort. Some tasks are simple and some are more complicated. But when you take on the task, you put in a certain amount of effort. So the question is, *how* do you do things? How would you describe the kind of effort you put into everything that you do?

Let's take a real-life example. Hopefully, at your age, you have been asked to do a few things around the house. Everyone can relate to taking out the garbage, even if you've never done it. If you have never taken out the garbage, you can compare this to any chore that you've done at your house, but for our purposes we're going to talk about taking out the trash.

How do you take out the garbage? Do you do it the first time you are asked or do you have to be asked several times? If you are taking care of the trash as soon as you are asked, good. You're perfectly capable and you're helping keep your house clean. You should feel good about that because you are contributing to a comfortable home. If you are being asked several times, let's think about that for a little bit.

Are you ignoring the requests because you want to live in a house full of trash? Yuck. This is doubtful. Who wants to live in a house surrounded by garbage? Are you not capable of taking out the trash? That is, is this a task that you cannot physically do? In this case, you should be considering a different task that you can contribute to help the order of your household. Are you hoping that the person asking you to take out the trash gets tired of asking you and does it themselves? What does this say about you?

Let's say that you finally take out the garbage. How do you do it? Do you check all the garbage cans and empty all of them? Clean anything that spills out of them or drops to the floor? Wipe the side of the can if there is anything on there that shouldn't be? After all, if you're not dirty or lazy then you would definitely want to take care of this in the best way possible. Or perhaps, after a lot of requests, you take out only one garbage bag, if anything falls out of it you leave it there, don't check any other place in the house and dump it in the outside garbage can. If everything goes in, great. If it doesn't, oh well, it will probably blow away. Right? Then it's not your problem. Do you put the trash out this way because you aren't capable of doing a better job of it? Probably not. Are you hoping that if someone nags you long enough and you do a lousy job of it, you'll never have to do it again?

So, although taking out the garbage might seem like a silly example, it is really a reflection about how you do everything. Once you start looking at tasks both simple and complicated as things that require your best effort, it changes how you see yourself. It also changes how you see the task. First, when you do something well (even small things) you feel good about yourself. That's growing your self-esteem. You improve your self-worth and see yourself as valuable. You grow your happiness because you contributed to the health and happiness of your family and home. You are kind because you helped others. When you decide to make an effort, you grow your ability to make the next effort. Over time you grow the habit of making your best effort on everything. When you grow this ability, you become a person people can count on to be helpful and get the job done. You will become someone who does not disappoint others and will simultaneously feel proud of yourself.

Does this sound simple? Yes. Easy? Maybe. With each small effort you make you change yourself into a person who is more capable and more valuable. That's an awesome way to be in the world, isn't it? Doing things that you are capable of so that you are valued and appreciated.

Think about what tasks are ahead of you today – school, home, work, or activities. How do you want to do them? You can be a burden or you can be appreciated. You can do them in a way that disappoints others and yourself or in a way that lets you like yourself as a person. Take a moment to be aware of how you feel about yourself once a job is done. It will make you want to do the next job even better.

Complete each box below.

| Think of a time someone did something for you in a way that showed they cared about you. How did you feel? | Think of a time someone did something for you in a way that was very uncaring. How did you feel? |
|---|---|
| Think of a time that you did something for someone that showed you cared about them. How did you feel? | Think of a time you did something for someone in a way that showed you were uncaring. How did you feel? |

The way it feels when someone does something in a way that shows they care about you is exactly how other people feel when you do something out of kindness for them. Notice on your chart how it feels when you are the recipient of a kind act. You have the power to help others feel that way about you just by the way you do things. Want to feel good about yourself? Watch how you do things.

**Finding Personal Success**

# Chapter 10

# What's Your Problem?

Take a moment to complete these questions.

What is currently your biggest problem? (You know, the one that first comes to mind, the problem that you really struggle with.)

_____

Why is this a problem for you?

_____

_____

_____

What are you doing about this problem?

_____

_____

_____

So, now that you have identified a problem and you know why it bothers you and what you are doing about it, let's consider two methods for solving this problem.

**Finding Personal Success**

First, you can think vertically. So, whatever you are doing about the problem, consider what would happen if you did it more often. What if you spent more time and energy doing the things that you are doing to solve the problem more consistently? Would this help improve the situation? I want to caution you that if your list of ways to deal with the problem includes things like "I'm doing nothing about it," "I'm complaining about it," or "I'm worrying about it," you might want to skip to the second method of problem solving. However, if you are doing some things that are aimed at reducing or eliminating the problem, but you're not doing them regularly, then you might want to start by using your solutions more frequently and consistently. Would this improve or eliminate your problem? If so, then start here and put your attention on these solutions.

Secondly, you can think horizontally. This is the opposite of thinking vertically. Instead of doing more of the same thing to solve the problem, you create new methods of solving the problem. If what you have been doing is not helping reduce or eliminate this problem, you need to stop doing it and do something else.

This is where you folks who were doing nothing, complaining, or worrying have to shift your focus. Here's the challenge – if you've been doing nothing, you're going to have to take ownership that the problem is yours and you are the only one who can do something about it. If you've been finding people to complain to, you're going to have to change your default setting and stop complaining. You might even want to ask people you trust for suggestions about how you can improve this situation. And if you're worrying, recognize that this is not ever going to help you get rid of this problem. In fact, wasting your energy worrying about it leaves you with less energy and totally blocks your mind from creating productive solutions.

Here's the thing about thinking horizontally. It assumes that every possible solution is equal. They are on the same plane. The only way to see which solution will improve your problem is to try one. Sometimes the simplest solution will be the most effective, and sometimes it won't be. You have to keep trying until you find the right fix. Another thing to consider when you are thinking horizontally is that your solution may be to change your mindset. If a person is bothering you, perhaps you are investing too much in that person's opinion or behavior. If something about your health is bothering you, you might have to change how you take care of your health – eat better, exercise, or stay away from toxic people. These changes require you to change something inside of you, rather than outside of you. Ultimately, every problem that you solve will require you to change something inside of yourself first, then your outside circumstances will improve.

Once you solve one problem, another will surely crop up. That's life. Your ability to solve your problems effectively is key to creating a happier and more successful life. Be prepared after you go through this process because you will have to repeat it over and over again. The good news is that solving your problems leaves you feeling good about yourself, which cannot be achieved by doing nothing, complaining, or worrying.

Look back at your biggest problem. Which method of problem solving seems like the best way to fix the issue? Horizontal or vertical?

Write down what you plan to do about the problem. If you are thinking horizontally, you might have to make a list of several possible actions you can take. (You can also ask family members or close friends to help you think of solutions.)

_____

_____

_____

_____

_____

_____

_____

_____

_____

_____

_____

# Chapter 11

# I Like Me, I Like Me Not

We all have moments where we like ourselves, and moments where we don't like ourselves very much. What makes the difference about how you feel about yourself in those moments? Is it the thoughts that you tell yourself in your head? Is it how you treat the people around you? Is it how the people around you treat you? In each of these moments we can tell ourselves positive and negative things, treat people well or poorly, and be treated well or poorly in return. These interactions, both in your head and with others, create how we feel about ourselves. This is called self-esteem.

When we have high self-esteem, we have positive thoughts and feelings about ourselves and when we have low self-esteem, we have negative thoughts and feelings about ourselves. Simple. But, if you've ever had a period of time where you did not feel very good about yourself and had negative thoughts about yourself, here are a few things you can do that can help you like yourself more.

1. Forgive everyone who has wronged you. Think of the people who have done little things and even people who have done big things that hurt your feelings. When people are negative toward others it's a sign that they don't like themselves. So, when they say or do mean things to you, it's probably not about you – it's about them. Everyone has to work through their own issues. Forgive them. It's a sign of maturity when you forgive someone else's mistake, poor judgment, or negative behavior. It doesn't mean allow someone to continue treating you poorly or hurting your feelings. It doesn't mean that you have to be their friend. It means allowing yourself to let it go and move on.
2. Forgive yourself. Apologize if you need to and move on. Everyone makes mistakes (see #1 above). So just as you forgive other people for their mistakes, forgive your own. However, if you have done something to hurt someone you need to apologize. Apologizing is important because it gives someone the opportunity to forgive you so you can improve the relationship you have with that

person. You will feel better about yourself because you have made the effort to correct something that you shouldn't have done. If the person you apologize to responds with anger or meanness, remember that you hurt them in some way and that can be difficult to get over. The apology is still the important thing. Whether or not they accept it is out of your control. Apologize anyway. The more you recognize that apologizing for your mistakes allows you to move forward, the better you become at forgiving others.

3. Begin each day with a confident statement. Today is going to be great. I am an amazing person. I am important. I believe in myself and I know I can do great things. Whatever speaks to you. Put it on your mirror, your dresser, your bedside table, your cell phone cover, wherever you will see it in the morning and several times throughout the day. Telling yourself something positive wires your brain to look for positive things in your day. Once your brain is looking for a positive day it will find one and you will feel better about yourself.

4. Stop comparing yourself to others. Everyone has strengths and weaknesses. You are better at some things than other people. Be humble. You are worse at some things than other people. Compliment them. No one excels at everything. Comparing yourself against others is a trap. Instead of falling into that trap, decide what you want to create that is all your own and spend your time doing that. You won't have time to compare it to anyone else and you will feel better about yourself. Write down what you are good at. Then write what you are not so good at. You can also ask a close friend or family member to help you with this list. You might be surprised at how they see you or what strengths you have that they recognize.

Take a few moments and write down some things that people have done to you that you need to let go of. Read each item over and realize that the moment is over and so is the unkind act. Let it go. Put it behind you. They may never apologize, but if you continue to carry it around, it's your burden.

_____

_____

_____

_____

_____

_____

_____

_____

Now write down some things that you've done that you wish you hadn't. Circle the ones that you still have the opportunity to apologize for. Now, figure out how you are going to say the words "I'm sorry" to that person. Remember that your goal is to like yourself better. No matter how hard it is at first, once you apologize, you'll feel better about yourself.

_____

_____

_____

_____

_____

_____

_____

Jot down some inspiring phrases that you can use to start your day. They can be a quote from someone famous, song lyrics that speak to you, or something you just made up. Remind yourself that you are on a mission to make choices that create an awesome life. You can even set them as a reminder that comes up on your phone every day.

_____

_____

_____

_____

_____

_____

Recognize that even someone who is the greatest person in the world at something is not the greatest at everything. So, no matter who you are and what you can do, there are some things you can do better than others and some things others can do better than you. Decide what you want to be great at and work at it. Invest the time and effort in creating a better you, and you won't have time to think about what everyone else is doing. Make a list of areas of your life you would like to improve. Next to each item, write why you want to change this for the better. Then you can decide how you can invest your time and energy to transform your life.

| What do I want to improve about myself or my life? | Why do I want to make this effort? | What are some things that I can do that will help me get started? |
| --- | --- | --- |
|  |  |  |
|  |  |  |
|  |  |  |
|  |  |  |
|  |  |  |

# Chapter 12

# Have You Ever Felt Unappreciated?

Have you ever given someone a gift or done something nice for someone, and they didn't appreciate it? They didn't say thank you. Perhaps they didn't acknowledge your kindness. What is the likelihood that you are going to give them another gift or do another kind deed for them?

Now think about this: Has anyone ever done something nice for you? Did you appreciate it? Drove you to practice or lessons? Sat at your game in the cold, rain, snow, heat, or wind? Explained something to you to help you understand it better? Sat through a three-hour dance recital to see you dance for 10 minutes? Made your favorite dinner? Kept you company when you weren't feeling well? Did your laundry? Vacuumed your room? Each of these acts of service is driven by kindness. Did you appreciate it? Did you notice it? Did you acknowledge it? Did you say, "Thank you"?

Have you ever had the experience of being driven somewhere by a parent or family member and they were resentful about doing it? You know, just cranky and complaining all the way to the place you had to go. Why do you think this happens? Could it be that these kind acts and acts of service that your parents, family, and friends are doing for you are going unappreciated? Most people would agree that if you do something nice for someone, you expect to be appreciated and if you don't feel appreciated, you're probably not going to do those nice things anymore. Yet, here are the people in your life driving you places, buying you things, taking care of you, and helping you get through your daily life a little more easily. Do you thank them? Do you express your genuine appreciation to them? Being happy they did it is not the same thing as saying, "Thank you for driving me to see my friend. I know you have other things you could be doing right now. I appreciate it."

Are you wondering how you can add the habit of gratitude to your day? Look for opportunities to say thank you. You can start by noticing small things. Thanks for dinner; it was delicious. Thanks for getting my favorite topping on the pizza. Thanks for going grocery shopping, I know that it's expensive and takes a lot of time and effort. Offer to go with them and help or carry in the groceries or help put them away. Give them a thank-you hug. If your family is not the hugging type, give them a hug – be the first to start a habit. It will be a powerful moment. Write them a thank-you note. You can text it too or put it where they will find it later. How you choose to show your gratitude is not the important part. Expressing your sincere appreciation is the important thing.

Beginning the habit of appreciating others and expressing gratitude is one of the most important things you can do to improve your life. It causes you to stop and realize how many things there are to be grateful for in a day. It grows your appreciation of others. It helps you feel better about yourself. It changes your outlook on people and things around you. And when you express gratitude to others, you will receive gratitude from others in return. This may not happen at first, but if you make it a habit to show your appreciation, gratitude will grow. Expressing thankfulness helps every aspect of your life. It makes a day that seems very difficult easier to get through. So, if you have been feeling unappreciated lately, you might begin by making the time to appreciate someone else.

Make a list of people who you are thankful to have in your life.

_____

_____

_____

_____

_____

Take a few minutes and write down some things that you are thankful for. Begin each sentence with "I am thankful for…" or "I am grateful for…"

_____

_____

_____

_____

_____

_____

_____

_____

_____

_____

Look over your list and find at least one thing that you could express appreciation for. Think of how you would tell someone how thankful you are for this particular thing. Make a plan to share your gratitude with someone today.

_____

_____

_____

_____

Look around your house or in your locker for an unused or lightly used notebook. Any size will do for this activity. Put this notebook and a pen that you like next to your bed. Every night before you go to sleep or every morning when you wake up, write down three things that you are thankful for. It seems like a small task but, it grows huge amounts of gratitude. The more often you practice reviewing your day and finding the moments that you are thankful for, the easier it is to find appreciation throughout your day and throughout your life.

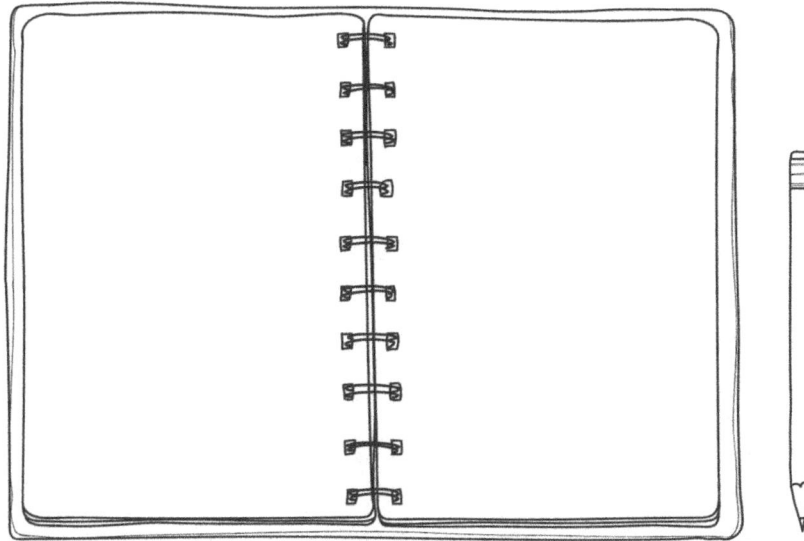

**Finding Personal Success**

# CHAPTER 13

# You Snooze, You Lose

When you start your day hitting the snooze button you are essentially starting your day with an excuse. An excuse not to get out of bed, not to get your day started, and to mentally complain about having been given this day. If you start your day by postponing the start of the day, it sets the mind in excuse mode. What else can I put off? I'll do that later, tomorrow, next week, someday. Check your calendar. There are no "somedays."

Here's an old saying that has a new application. "You snooze, you lose" can mean that if you sit back and do nothing, you will be missing out on a lot of opportunities. This old saying has a new way of being applied to life. If you have a smartphone that you use as an alarm, it has a snooze button that you can hit that will let you plop down in bed for another nine minutes before it sounds again. Did you know that you can disable the snooze button on your smartphone? You can turn it off in your alarm settings. The company that made your phone has a snooze button set to ON as a default. They anticipate that people will use their snooze alarm and are basically saying, "Hey, procrastinators! We got you! Yup, just hit snooze and lay there and make excuses not to get out of bed. It's fine. Don't get motivated. See you in nine minutes."

If you start the day with a go-get-it-done attitude, you will have a day where you get things done. If you start the day with an excuse, you'll spend the day making excuses for yourself instead of making an effort that leads to progress. Here's a tip, before you go to sleep at night, get in the practice of making a list of goals for the next day. It wires your brain to go achieve those goals. So, it's in your best interest to turn off your snooze button and put your mind in goal achieving mode instead of excuses and procrastination mode. Grab your list of goals, read it, and get going.

Science tells us that it is harder to stop a habit than it is to replace habit. So, if you want to have days where you feel successful, then you need to stop making excuses. Replace excuses with a list of what you want to accomplish. Replace your snooze button with something that inspires you. Pick a theme song and make it your alarm. Make sure it makes you smile and energizes you. Let it motivate you! Transform your procrastination into productivity and have an amazing day!

Use the chart on the next page to get you started.

Fill in the boxes with your answers.

| Number 1 thing I would really like to do: | Number 2 thing I would really like to do: | Number 3 thing I would really like to do: |
|---|---|---|
| What excuse am I making that is stopping me from doing this? | What excuse am I making that is stopping me from doing this? | What excuse am I making that is stopping me from doing this? |
| What is one thing (or two or three) that I can change that would override my excuse? | What is one thing (or two or three) that I can change that would override my excuse? | What is one thing (or two or three) that I can change that would override my excuse? |
| How will it feel when I accomplish this goal? | How will it feel when I accomplish this goal? | How will it feel when I accomplish this goal? |

**Finding Personal Success**

# The Domino Effect

Before you read this chapter, write down one thing that you wish was different about your life.

_____

_____

_____

_____

_____

Have you ever seen an elaborate set-up of dominoes where someone knocks down the first domino and then a series of toppling dominoes making twists and turns follows? Pretty neat. Life is like this. Every time you make a move, a series of moves follow. In fact, people can often look back at a decision they made or an action they took and connect it to how they got to where they are right now. Whether they are in a good place or in a tough spot can be a result of that one choice.

Think about your life. Do you like everything just the way it is or is there something you would like to be different? If you could change your life in one way, what would you change? One thing. Maybe you don't like how you get along with a particular person? Maybe you don't like how school is going? Maybe you want to find something more interesting to do with your free time? Whatever it is, imagine how your life would improve if you had this one change in your life.

**Finding Personal Success**

A lot of people believe that if they sit back, someone else or something else will change and then their life will get better. (If only my parents would get off my back. If only my brother would be nicer to me. If only I could have this one thing, my life would get better.) With this belief is the risk that someone or something else has the power and the ability to choose the direction of your life. Sitting back allows someone else's actions to control your life or your circumstances.

Imagine this situation if you were riding a bike. You are pedaling and someone else is in charge of moving the handlebars. You have no idea where you are going because you've put that in someone else's hands. You just keep pedaling not knowing what's coming up ahead or whether or not you should speed up or slow down. You have no say in where you end up because you have handed over that decision to whoever has control of your handlebars. You could go to the beach or off the edge of a cliff. And you just pedal.

This seems like a silly scenario, how can you let someone else steer your bike? You have no idea where you'll end up. But this is exactly what happens when you don't like something in your life and you sit back and wait for someone else to do something about it. You keep pedaling through your days and you let the people and circumstances around you decide how your life ends up.

Living your life this way allows you to complain about everything until, ultimately, you believe that you don't have the power to change your life or control your future. Along with the belief that you can't change your own life circumstances, there is also the idea that you cannot change anything in your circle of friends or your community or the world. If you would rather spend your time complaining and making excuses about life while other people go places and do things, then be prepared to meet with a lot of disappointment when things don't go your way.

Taking hold of the handlebars means you should be prepared to decide where you want to go in life and how fast you want to get there. It requires you to think about what you want your life to look like and then make choices that keep you going in the direction that best serves you. This choice is called your domino. This domino represents how one change can affect everything else in your life. It is the toppling of one domino that can set everything else in motion. You can wish and hope for someone else to change or you can make the first move.

Here's the hard part. What? You thought that making your life better was easy? You have to let go of the belief that you can't change something. Stop putting the direction of your life in someone else's hands. Stop sitting around waiting for things to just get better. Stop making excuses. Do you want a better relationship with someone? Be nicer to them. Decide what you want the relationship to look like and act the way you want to be treated. Do you want to do better in school, sports, or music? What would that take? Get help? Practice with more intention? You know the answer. You just might be stuck in a place where you don't want to change. Change isn't hard.

Deciding that you want something badly enough to change what you are doing – that's hard. Making a shift in thinking is the first step to moving that first domino. Once you choose where you want to apply your time, effort, and intention you can lean in and push your first domino. When it falls, something else will follow and another thing and another. Be prepared for your life to start looking a lot more like you want it to. But recognize that your life will also be in your hands, so you will have no one else to blame and no one to complain to about your choices. Everything that happens will be on your shoulders, which means that when your life is great, you will be the cause of that.

Look back at what you wrote before you read this chapter. Based on what you want to change, write down at least one thing you can do today to start your domino effect. Choose something that is entirely within your control.

_____

_____

_____

_____

_____

_____

_____

# Guilty or Innocent

What's the difference between feeling guilty or not guilty? Think about a time that you did something that you felt guilty about. It's not a good feeling. Here's why.

We all live by a set of standards. Being human, we have to accept that each person is living by a different set of standards. For example, what does it mean when you say you can keep a secret? Does it mean that you will not tell another person what was said to you in confidence? Or you will tell only your best friend, your sibling, or maybe just your inner circle of friends? When someone trusts you enough to tell you their secret, the assumption is that you share the same standard for this exchange. If the person shares something very personal to them and you both understand that no one else can hear this secret, you have a bond that you both understand. However, when you share your secret and the person you trust with this secret has a different standard of keeping a secret – and they only tell one friend, or one small group of friends – this can feel like betrayal. They have broken a trust, and depending on the size of the secret, they may have shattered a friendship too. Why did this happen? Because you and that person did not have the same set of standards.

It's important to write down our standards and really examine our boundaries. How honest are you? How trustworthy are you? What are your goals and what are you willing to do achieve them? How do you treat people? What behavior will you accept from others and what won't you tolerate?

Writing this down can be very eye opening. You might come to a realization about yourself that would inspire you to make some changes. You can also define your boundaries and stop allowing people to take advantage of you.

Once you solidify your standards in your mind (and on paper), this becomes the tool that measures whether you are guilty or innocent. If you break your own standards, you feel guilty. If you believe that a secret should never be told and breaking that confidence is betrayal, when you tell that secret to someone else, you feel guilty. If you believe that everyone should be treated equally, then when you make fun of someone or belittle them in some way, you feel guilty. You've broken your own standards.

It happens. What do you do when you're guilty? First, sincerely apologize if you can. The guilt will melt away and you'll be less frustrated at what you did. Recognize that that person may or may not forgive you. It depends on their standards. Second, learn the lesson and forgive yourself. Third, don't repeat it.

How do you want to spend your time, feeling guilty or feeling innocent? Use the questions that follow to help you define some of your standards. No one else is going to see this, so just be honest with yourself.

How honest am I?

___

___

___

How trustworthy am I?

___

___

___

How do I treat people?

___

___

___

What will I absolutely not tolerate from other people, under any circumstances?

___

___

___

What am I willing to do to get what I want?

_____
_____
_____
_____

What am I not willing to do to get what I want?

_____
_____
_____
_____

What are some personal standards that I hold myself to without anyone telling me what's right or wrong?

_____
_____
_____
_____

Do I hold other people to these standards too?

_____
_____
_____

How do I respond when other people don't measure up to my standards?

_____
_____
_____

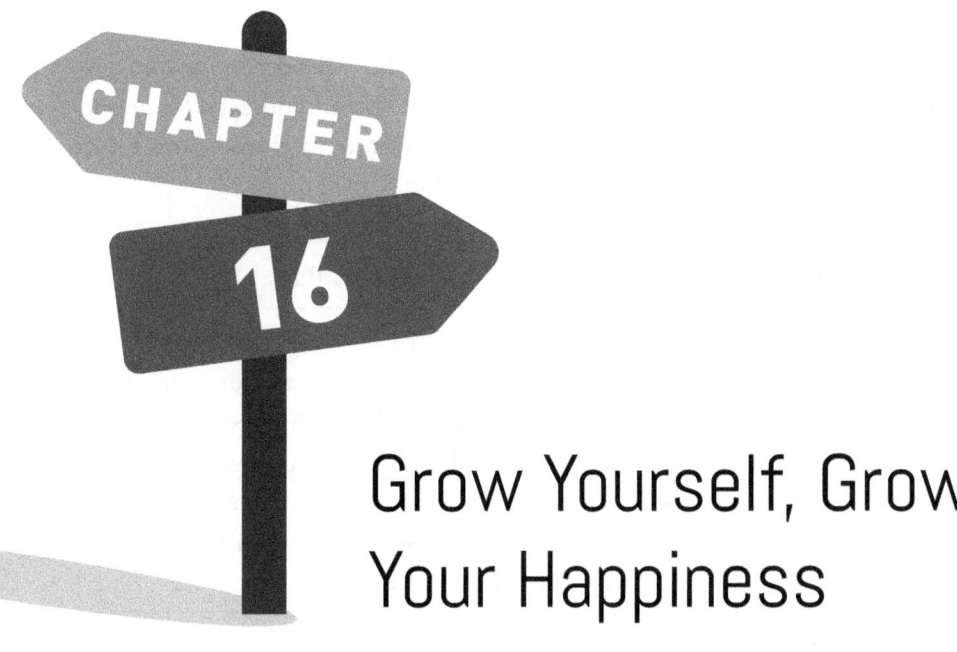

# Grow Yourself, Grow Your Happiness

Before you read this chapter, make a list of about 10 things that you have done in the past few days. This is a list of things that you have done. Do not list things that have happened to you.

_____
_____
_____
_____
_____
_____
_____
_____
_____
_____

**Finding Personal Success**

Remember that food pyramid you learned about in health class? It puts all the different foods into categories based on how much you should eat of those foods. There's some that you should eat a lot of and then some that you should only consume in small amounts. There's simpler way to think about food. Instead of the complicated names and categories, here is a simplified version.

|  | Tastes Good | Tastes Bad |
|---|---|---|
| Good For you | In this category you can put the foods that you like that are healthy for you. Strawberries, apples, tomatoes, chicken soup – whatever healthy foods that you like. If you eat these all the time, it will have a positive effect on your health. | In this category you put the foods that you don't particularly care for, but they are still good for you. Maybe you don't like Brussel sprouts or asparagus but they are good for you. Any healthy food that would not be something you request for dinner can go here. |
| Bad For You | In this category you put the foods that are bad for you but that taste good. Things like potato chips, French fries, candy, soda – you get the idea. You want to eat these, but they are not very good for your health. If you eat these all the time, it will have a negative effect on you. | In this category you put the foods that taste bad and are bad for you. Nobody wants to eat these foods. Spoiled food, overcooked food, undercooked food, and anything that does not taste good and is not good for your health goes in this category. There aren't very many foods that go in this category. Eating them is definitely not good for your health. |

So, the thing about this system is that is also works for our actions. Consider the list that you made a few minutes ago. Instead of fitting those items into a food pyramid, let's look at a system like the one above and examine our actions.

|  | Feels Good | Feels Bad |
|---|---|---|
| Good For you | In this category you put the actions that feel good and are good for you.<br><br>Some examples are: playing sports, going to bed early, being outside in good weather, laughing, being kind to someone, spending time with friends, listening to music. Any positive activity that brings you joy and doesn't hurt others are all things that feel good and are good for you.<br><br>**This box is your happiness.** | In this category you put the actions that feel bad and are good for you.<br><br>Some examples are making mistakes, doing chores, apologizing, asking for help, and doing a job without expecting to be thanked or rewarded. No one likes to make mistakes, but that's how you learn. Some people have a hard time apologizing. These people also think they never make mistakes. When you're stuck in this pattern, it's hard to grow and improve yourself. Asking for help actually makes you aware that everyone needs help sometimes and it gives someone else the opportunity to feel good by doing something nice (the box to the left). Some other examples are: losing a game because it increases your sportsmanship, doing homework and studying because it increases your ability to learn, and for some people eating vegetables because it helps your body feel better. **This box is your growth.** |
| Bad For You | In this category you put the actions that feel good and are bad for you.<br><br>Some pretty unhealthy things fall in this category. Underage drinking, vaping, smoking, procrastinating, revenge, retaliation, saying, "I told you so." In the moment, you might think you look cool smoking or drinking alcohol, but in the long run it's not good for you. You might also think it's okay to seek revenge on someone who has offended you in some way, but it just makes you as mean as they are. Feels good in the moment, but grows some really unhealthy feelings. By the way, anything that includes violence that you are using for entertainment falls in this category. Some other examples are staying up too late, eating a lot of junk food, being lazy when people are counting on you, bullying and trash talking. **This box is where you break your character.** | In this category you put the actions that feel bad and are bad for you.<br><br>Actions like being mean to others bring out the less attractive side of you and they also send negative messages to the inside of you. When you pretend you can't do something so you won't have to – you can load the dishwasher, do the laundry, or rake leaves. When you do a lousy job hoping no one asks you to do it again. Here's some other examples: getting sick (usually due to not eating or sleeping properly), telling lies, getting angry, worrying, and complaining.<br><br>**This box is where you need to change if you want to have a longer list in your happiness box.** |

Now that you have read this chart, look at the blank chart on the next page. Fill it in with the items on your list from the beginning of this chapter. How many of your activities can you put in each of the categories?

|            | Feels Good | Feels Bad |
|------------|------------|-----------|
| Good for you |          |           |
| Bad for you  |          |           |

How many of your activities can you put in the "Feel Good, Good for You" category? Can you think of anything you could do that would fit into that category and improve how much happiness you have?

_____

_____

_____

_____

How about the "Feels Good, Bad for You" category? This is where you make a lot of growth with just a few small changes. What are some positive changes you could make to transform these actions into actions that would move your actions into the "Feels Good, Good for You" category? Usually this requires just a small shift in habits.

___

How about the "Feels Bad, Good for you"? Here's another area where you can stretch yourself and grow. What are some things you could do to help you add to this category?

___

Finally, the "Feels Bad, Bad for You" category. When you stop doing these things not only do you become a better person, you like yourself a lot more. What would inspire you to make better choices for your actions?

___

Being an honest, productive, and positive person makes you nice to be around. What's good for you is that people who are honest, productive, and positive want to be around you too. When you're in a spot where you don't know what to do, ask yourself which category your actions would fall into. Aim for the action that will allow you to grow yourself, grow your happiness, and build your character in a positive way.

# Living Large

Imagine that you have been invited to a royal palace. What does it look like? When you go inside what do you see? Is it filled with beautiful things or is it filled with junk? Is it dirty or clean? Royalty knows how to live. They have only beautiful things in their palace, and they keep it very clean. They surround themselves with the best of everything.

Now consider your body. It's where you are going to live for the rest of your life. You will take it everywhere you go, and what you do with it will always be with you. It is your palace. Are you taking care of it like it is a palace? What would that look like? Would you eat junk food or healthy food? Would you build it to make it strong or would you let it fall into a crumbling structure? When you realize that your body is going to be with you for the rest of your life, you think carefully about what you are doing to and with your body. Making healthy food choices makes your body clean on the inside and your skin clear on the outside. Moving your body makes it able to perform in a way that lets you feel good. You don't have to go to the gym every day and grow giant muscles to have a body that will work for you, but if you sit around all day and wonder why you're tired, it's because your body isn't in the habit of doing anything for you.

Let's talk about your mind. If you plan to have it with you for the rest of your life – and hopefully you do – what are you putting in your mind? Are you filling it with beautiful things or garbage? Are you exercising it with learning new things or letting it crumble and become stagnant? What are you thinking about? Do you spend the day worrying, gossiping, complaining, or talking about negative things? That's like filling your house with trash. Do you spend time creating – art, music, writing, games, laughter? That's like filling your palace with beauty.

If you want your life to be first-class, you have to fill your life with the finest things. You can start by eating the healthiest foods that are available to you. If you aren't already making time to exercise or be active, find something you enjoy and make time to get involved with that. Positive thinking is essential to creating a healthy mind. These things are not always easy. However, living in a broken down and crumbling body is no easy thing either. Step by step you can build the body and mind you want to live in for the rest of your life.

Write down three things that you could do to take better care of yourself.

| One way you could change what you eat. (Either start eating something or stop eating something.) | One way you could change how you move. (Change the amount of exercise you are doing or change the amount of movement you have in your daily activities.) | One way you could change how you think. (What positive thing can you add to your thoughts or what negative thing can you subtract from your thoughts?) |
|---|---|---|
| How would this change affect your life? | How would this change affect your life? | How would this change affect your life? |

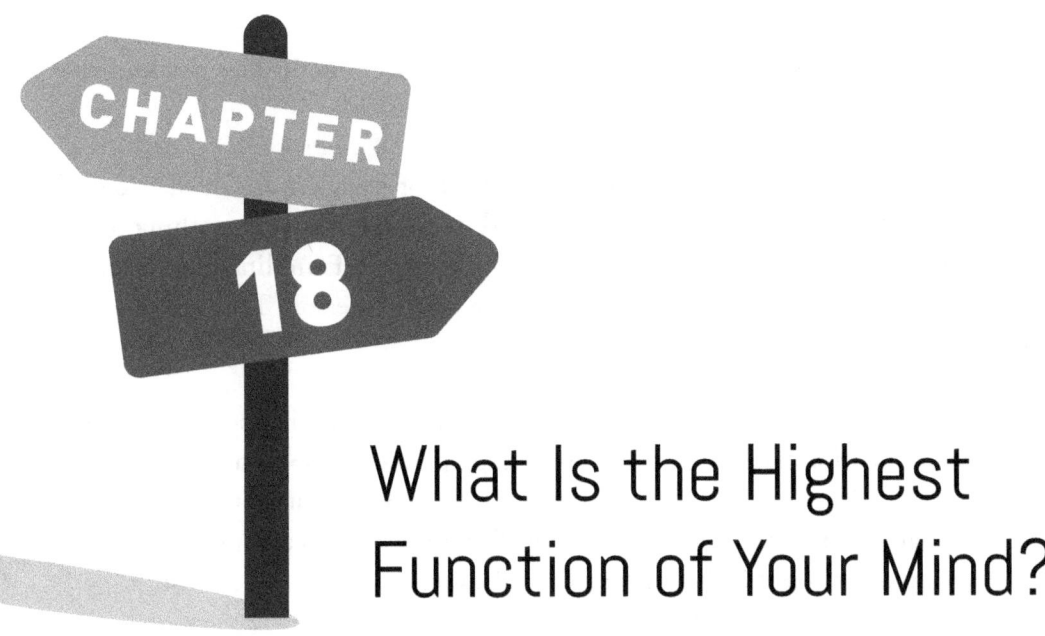

# What Is the Highest Function of Your Mind?

Creativity is the highest function of the mind. It is also the highest form of excellence. Creativity is when you use your mind to make something that has never existed before. Creativity is when inspiration and focused effort combine. Once you are inspired by something, hard work is still required in order for you to make something new.

The world likes conformity, and sometimes it's necessary. In school, people need rules such as forming lines, a behavior code, directions on academic assignments, and maybe even a dress code. Some of these rules apply out in the real world too. There's a general set of guidelines for what is appropriate behavior and so there are laws. People stand in line and wait their turn because it is a fair and civilized way to get things done. Creativity, on the other hand, is the urge to do something different, something that is not a repetition of what someone else has done. Creative people often have a difficult time with rules. They like to think about things differently and don't necessarily want to do things in ways that have been done before. Sometimes these people are described as people who like to color outside the lines or think out of the box.

People who are creative have a strong desire to lead an uncommon life. They want to use their potential to make life more interesting. Instead of having the same routine every day, they like innovation. Perhaps they frequently use a different route to get home, try something they've never eaten before at restaurants, or would rather make up their own song instead of practicing the same one over and over.

There was once a scientist who took a particular species of caterpillar and conducted an experiment. The caterpillars had the instinct to follow each other in a line to get food. The scientist placed the caterpillars on the edge of a round flowerpot. In the flowerpot was the caterpillars' main food source. The insects followed each other around the rounded edge until they eventually starved to death. That's conformity.

Following everyone else and doing exactly what they are doing is also conformity. It does not lead to new ideas.

Thankfully, human beings can make choices about following the crowd or stepping out in their own direction. A few examples of people who refused to follow the crowd in order to create something new include such individuals as Steve Jobs, Bill Gates, Leonardo da Vinci, Benjamin Franklin, and Thomas Edison. Virtually every singer, songwriter, artist, author, and CEO is a creative person. Their inventions and abilities gave us something that never existed before.

Everyone has something that would allow them to show their creativity. Not all of it happens in school. One person might be able to create new foods and recipes and excel at preparing delicious meals. Another person might be able to make art, music, or stories with their creativity. Someone else might invent a new trick in skateboarding or snowboarding. It's different for everybody. But using your creativity by focusing on what inspires you and working on a project is the highest form of using the power of your mind.

Here are some questions for you to consider about creativity. Your answers might just reveal where your creative talents lie.

How do I deal with change?

___

___

___

___

___

___

How often do I change things in my routine to make life more interesting?

___

___

___

___

___

___

What would I like to change about my routine?

___

Do I like doing what everybody else is doing? Why or why not?

___

What do I like to do that I would like to expand on and do differently?

___

What am I so comfortable doing that if I had to change it up it wouldn't be a problem for me?

___

What creative interests do I have?

_____
_____
_____
_____
_____

If I could create one thing, what would it be and why would I focus on creating it?

_____
_____
_____
_____
_____
_____
_____

# Chapter 19

# Who Would You Bet On?

Imagine that you could choose one person and follow that person for the rest of their life. Along with following this person, you would get 10 percent of what they earn for the rest of your life. Who would you bet on? Your choice would determine how much money you make and you would probably want to choose the person who you think would be the most successful. Many people would choose the person with the highest grades. It is a fallacy that the person who achieves the highest grades is the most successful and earns the most money. Some of you would choose your best friend. Being likeable is not always an indicator of a person's success. Here's the thing there are specific qualities that the most successful people use to their advantage.

Warren Buffet is a very rich man. He does not manufacture anything, he does not provide any service, and he does not own any corporation. How did he get so rich? Warren Buffet invests his money in people and takes a percentage of what they earn. So, how did he get rich? He has to decide whom he wants to invest in. If you are deciding whom you should bet on, here are some criteria to consider.

First and most importantly, invest in people with integrity. People who are willing to say "no" to things that are not in their best interest and have boundaries and a set of principles that they live by are a good bet. Integrity is defined by how honest you are and how often you choose to do the right thing. The amount of time you spend doing what is important to you reveals a lot about your integrity. One way to cultivate your integrity is to write for five to ten minutes a day. Write down things that you observe, things that are important to you and make connections between your ideas to increase your understanding of the world and refine your main beliefs. This helps you define what you find interesting and important and set aside time for those things. It also sets some boundaries so you can define what is not important to you so you don't waste time on those activities or with certain people. Decide what you want and then say "no" to the things that aren't going to help you get it.

**Finding Personal Success**

People you should bet on are energetic. This means they take care of their health, they exercise, they get enough sleep, eat healthy, and have a purpose that they believe in so they can put their energy into it. They don't get sick often and when they do, they recover quickly. They don't let large things overwhelm them; they take it one step at a time and focus their energy on what they can do right now to move forward.

The most successful people also have adaptive intelligence. They are willing to change and adapt as the situations around them change. In this society, things are changing at a rapid pace. When things change, the one who is going to continue to be successful is the person who can adapt to the changes and use their energy and their principles to keep them moving in a successful direction. When problem arise, they determine the best way to address the problem while keeping their integrity and goals in mind. They focus their energy and adapt to the situation.

So, in the end, when you consider whom you would bet on if your future depended on it, you shouldn't look for someone else. You should look in a mirror. As you get older, get out of school, and move on with your life, these people who are your friends now will very likely not be around. They will have gone off in their own direction to build their own future. You are the only one you can count on to create your success. Ask yourself, "Am I saying no to things that waste my time and energy? Am I spending my time and energy on activities and with people who are making me a better person? Am I taking care of myself so that I am able to have choices about what I want to do with my life? Am I willing to change my mind and continue to learn? Am I willing to hold on to my values and solve problems in ways that best serve me?" If you answered yes to these questions, you are making an investment in yourself. Your future success depends on it.

What do you do that shows your integrity? What do you say "no" to because it is not the choice that will lead you in the direction you want to go?

_____

_____

_____

_____

What are some ways you can take better care of your health and keep up your energy level?

_____

_____

_____

How do you respond when things change? Do you panic, get irritated, or go with the flow?

_____
_____
_____
_____
_____

How do you respond to changes in your daily routine or your environment?

_____
_____
_____
_____

If you have a difficult time with change or surprises, what would it take for you to adapt or change your response to the situation?

_____
_____
_____
_____

How do you respond when you are faced with a problem?

_____
_____
_____
_____

# CHAPTER 20

# Deliberate Time

Time is an interesting thing. You can't touch it or see it, but everybody wants it. Even though everybody has it, they want more of it. Why do they want more of it? How do you use our time? Most people want more time to do the things they love. The trick to creating more time is knowing how to slow it down. We spend so many hours of our day in a constant state of distraction. We check social media, email, text messages, watch TV, play video games, and then worry about what everybody else is doing. The day is a blur of small increments of time that are disconnected from each other. How can you create more time from this sea of distraction?

The key to creating more time is focus. In Chapter 4, we discussed becoming an expert through deliberate practice of a particular thing. The word deliberate is the important thing. When you do something deliberately, you are focused. We experience focus on the playing field, the orchestra, the hiking trail, or wherever you go to do your favorite activity. In those moments of intense focus, the rest of the world falls away. You can't hear the crowd cheering, the lawn mower next door, someone calling you from the other room or the noise that usually crowds your mind. When you are totally engrossed in a project that you enjoy, your social media, hungry stomach, and distractions disappear. Time flies so quickly that you look up in surprise when the whistle blows for the end of the game or you reach the end of the trail or someone calls you for dinner. Why? Because you have been so intent on your idea or interest that you could not be distracted. Working this way has been shown, through scientific measurement, to decrease how many hours it takes to become an expert at something. Sometimes the time is decreased by up to half of what it takes to learn something in the midst of distraction.

Focus gives you the opportunity to build something bigger than yourself. You start with an idea and you focus on it. The hard work involved seems to flow effortlessly. Your creativity expands as one step in the process seems to flow into the next step. Your energy seems limitless. This is focus, and it creates a flow of creativity. So, how do you get into this flow?

First, forget popularity. Don't focus on things that you think will make you look better to other people. You'll be wasting your time and you aren't being authentic to your own interests.

Second, let go of things that clutter your life and take up your time with distractions. These distractions actually get in the way of you being the best version of yourself. These interruptions can be material things like the stuff in your closet that you don't want or use anymore that keep you from finding what you need. They can be electronic distractions like having every notification turned on so your phone is constantly interrupting your attention. Perhaps you can think of other things that get you off course from your goals.

Third, let go of anger and grudges. The emotion of anger steals your creative energy and fills you with destructive energy.

Fourth, seek your own greatness. There is enough greatness for everybody. When you get to think of anything you want to without anyone telling you what to think, where does your mind go? If your mind goes there a lot, get curious and start experimenting with this area of interest. It might be a step in the direction of what you will be great at.

Fifth, stop wasting time with the thousands of activities that keep you from doing what makes you happy. Once time is gone, you can't get it back. Do you really want to spend it watching what other people are doing and posting on social media, or do you want to go do great things?

Finally, surround yourself with people who support you, who want you to be great, and who are positive influences.

Think about the following questions. See if anything turns up that helps you focus.

Have you ever had the experience of being really productive on a project and having time fly? You were so focused on what you were doing that you didn't realize that a large amount of time had passed? What productive activity were you doing?

_____

_____

_____

_____

How do you feel when you are focused on something that seemed effortless?

_____
_____
_____
_____

What did you accomplish during this period of time? What was the quality of that work?

_____
_____
_____
_____
_____
_____

When your mind wanders, what do you think about? It doesn't matter what other people think about. You are in charge of your life, so focus on your constructive interests.

_____
_____
_____
_____

What would it feel like to be an expert in this interest of yours? How would it affect your life?

_____
_____
_____
_____

# CHAPTER 21

# Beware of Vampires!

You're walking at the mall, and you see a person with a black leather jacket, a black t-shirt, and motorcycle boots. They have a long beard, sunglasses, and chains on their wrists and hanging from their belt. You assume that this person is part of a motorcycle gang or perhaps that they are mean. That's a judgment. You don't know anything about them. They might be the nicest person you'll ever meet, but you have judged them without much information. Unfortunately, people judge others like this all the time. School can be an especially difficult place to avoid being judged. Everyone has an opinion about how others should dress and act. People fall into the trap of doing what the most popular kids think they should do instead of being themselves.

Let's get away from judgment and talk about evaluating people. For our purposes, let's consider that people can be put in three categories. People can be positive, neutral, or negative. When you interact with a positive person, you feel uplifted. They raise your spirits and you leave their company feeling happier than before you interacted with them. You like to be around these people because you go away feeling cheerful. Then, there are neutral people. When you interact with them you don't feel any change in how you feel. The interaction was neither positive nor negative. Finally, there are negative people. These people leave you feeling drained after interacting with them. They are constantly looking for someone to complain to, who will listen to their problems and join their pity party for whatever crisis they think has overtaken them. After you leave them, you think, "Man, that was exhausting." And it is, because they suck the energy out of you. They drain away your happiness and positive outlook. The problem is that by taking in your energy, they feed their own negativity. These people are looking to spread their negative outlook and like vampires, they're never satisfied, they are always looking for their next victim.

Everyone gets a certain amount of energy each day. We sleep and when we wake up, hopefully rested, we have enough energy to go about our day and do the things we need to do and the things we like to do.

We also get energy from the food that we eat. Along with this certain amount of energy, which is limited, we have a certain number of days too. We might not like to think about that, but it's true. So, now you have to decide what you are going to do with your energy today. Are you going to spend it with positive people who make you feel happy, or with negative people who are going to drain the life out of you?

Using your energy to your greatest advantage takes some evaluation of the people and circumstances you are interacting with each day. Consider the big picture of your experiences with each person. Let's say you've interacted with someone 25 times and 24 of those times you felt exhausted. You have evaluated this after many interactions and determined that this person in an energy vampire. One exception is, if you've been friends with someone for a long time and they are usually uplifting, you should avoid judging them if they are going through a difficult situation or illness. This can make them sad, worried or anxious. They can complain to you, but it's temporary and they need your support and friendship, not your judgment. If, on the other hand, you spend time with someone and 24 out of 25 times you feel happy and uplifted, you can safely evaluate this person as a positive influence in your life.

Now, the law of conservation of energy says that energy cannot be created or destroyed. So, each day you wake up and you have a certain amount of energy. You can spend it doing anything, but you only have the amount of energy that you get from getting sleep at night, exercising, and eating properly. So, you have to decide how you are going to use your energy each day. Here's where you need to be aware of energy vampires. How do you deal with them? You want to be kind, considerate, and honest. First, don't engage with them. Don't say, "How are you?" Because you don't want to hear them complain, and you aren't invested in how they are because you do not want to listen to their negative comments and complaints. Say something like, "Hello. Isn't this a nice day? If you would excuse me, I have something important I need to do. I hope you have a good day." You've avoided having your energy drained. You were honest: "I have something important to do" – get on with your life and conserve your energy because you only have a finite amount of energy. You were kind: "Isn't this a nice day?" And you were compassionate; you do hope that they have a good day. You've saved your energy for positive things and have energy to spend on the things that are important to you.

When you are not sure if someone is draining you of your energy, just become aware of how you feel before you see them and then after you spend some time with them. Usually a few interactions will give you some perspective on whether you want to spend more of your time and energy in their company.

Time for a little self-reflection.

Think about how you approach your day. Are you a snooze-button enthusiast? Do you have a tendency to complain about things? What kind of attitude about life are you walking around with these days?

_____

_____

_____

_____

What behaviors do you take part in regularly that are serving you well? Are they creating positive energy for you and those around you?

_____

_____

_____

_____

How could you increase the frequency of these actions?

_____

_____

_____

_____

What behaviors do you take part in regularly that are not serving you well? How are they creating negative energy for you and those around you?

_____

_____

_____

_____

How could you decrease the frequency of these actions?

_____

_____

_____

_____

# CHAPTER 22

# It's Not What You Look at That Matters, It's What You See

This chapter title is actually a quote from Henry David Thoreau. Another way of saying this is when you change the way you look at things, the things you look at change. Hold up your hand and look at it. Do you see five fingers? Actually, the number you see is nine. You see five fingers and four spaces between your fingers. Take a moment and be thankful for your five fingers and the fact that they have spaces between them. You may have never thought of your hand this way before. We're grateful for what our fingers can do, but we should then also appreciate that each finger can move independently, and they have a space between them. Otherwise we would not be able to do many of the things we enjoy. We are thankful for what is there and what is not there. That is what makes the whole.

Let's take this a little further. What makes a tree? The leaves and branches? Or the leaves, branches, and the space between them? Imagine music and all the notes. What makes it music? The notes? Or the notes and space between the notes? If you played all the notes at once, it wouldn't be music. What makes you? Everything you are? Or everything you are and everything you are not?

Think about the world around you. What makes it beautiful or meaningful or enjoyable? Everything it is? Or everything it is and everything it is not? Why do you like your friend? For who they are? Or for who they are and who they are not? Think about someone or something that you love. What is it about that person or thing that allows you love them? What is it about that person or thing that they are not that allows you to love them? This shift in perspective opens your mind and helps you see things from a broader viewpoint.

Now, think of something you don't like very much. Why don't you like it? Is it because of what it is or what it is not? Instead of thinking of things as good or bad, positive or negative, what if you looked at them as the whole thing – what's there and what's missing. Doing this helps us find the value of everyone, everything, and every situation, both for the things we experience that help us and the things that challenge us. When we start considering everything from the whole perspective, it helps us appreciate things more fully. Considering the whole perspective means that you will step back and see a person, thing, situation, or idea in its entirety. It means that you will consider all the characteristics of that person, thing, or idea. It also makes it easier to get through difficult situations because we recognize that there are a whole set of circumstances not just one side to the story. Often once a difficult situation has passed, we can reflect on it and see how what at first appeared to be unpleasant actually was beneficial.

Write down one thing that you like.

_____

_____

_____

What does it have that makes you like it?

_____

_____

_____

What doesn't it have that allows you to like it?

_____

_____

_____

Write down one thing that you do not like.

_____

_____

_____

What does it have that causes you not like it?

_____

_____

_____

What is missing that keeps you from liking it?

_____

_____

_____

When you change your perspective, many things that you might otherwise think of as negative, are actually positive; they might just not be to your benefit.

Think of a situation that you perceive as being difficult. Step back and look at the whole thing. Consider your side of the situation and the other person's side of the situation.

What part of the situation is to your benefit?

_____

_____

_____

Which part of the situation does not benefit you?

_____

_____

_____

Is the part that is not benefiting you benefiting someone else? How?

_____

_____

_____

# Imagination is Everything

Among many other things, Albert Einstein said, "Imagination is everything." As one of the leading minds in physics, Einstein recognized that in order to invent things or solve problems you need to use your imagination. Your imagination can think of one idea and that one idea can lead to countless others. The best thing about the creation of ideas is it is limitless. Imagination is also free, so it is available to everyone equally. You can think of ideas that are random or a group of ideas that lead you to accomplishing one goal or solving one problem. The most effective way to have ideas bring you success is to have a clearly defined goal.

Setting a goal for something you want to achieve is key to growing your imagination. Answer each of the following questions to see how your imagination can be harnessed for your success.

Choose one habit in your life that is not serving you well. Think of something that you are doing or not doing that is not in your best interest. Write this down here.

_____

_____

Explain why you are doing this. Knowing why you are doing something is key to changing a behavior.

_____

_____

_____

**Finding Personal Success**

What could you be doing instead?

_____

_____

_____

How could you change what you are doing?

_____

_____

_____

What is one thing (or two or three) that you could do differently to change this habit?

_____

_____

_____

How could this change affect your life?

_____

_____

_____

_____

How would it feel if your imagination helped you transform this habit?

_____

_____

_____

_____

You just used your imagination to create one way that you could potentially solve a problem or enrich your life. A healthy imagination looks to improve things, not destroy them. Imagination sees how things could be. Your mind has enough imagination to solve your problems, but it needs to be directed by you toward whatever goal you set. Your imagination can combine, rearrange, and reverse ideas. It helps if you stay away from people who tell you your ideas are no good. Your imagination exercises your mind and builds your ability to improve your life.

Here is a list of things that help grow your imagination so that it can best serve you.

1. Ask questions – about what you are doing and about what others are doing.
2. Appreciate other people's ideas – don't just ignore them or shut them down because of whose idea it is. Keep an open mind.
3. Your imagination would like you to keep a pen and paper handy. Research shows that once you have an idea you have about 5 seconds to act on it. If the time to act isn't now, write it down so you can act on it later.
4. Talk to others about their ideas and interests.
5. Change your mindset and instead of having problems, have challenges. Once you are successful in the challenge, you will feel like a winner.
6. Stop worrying or complaining and instead invest your time and energy into finding solutions.
7. Prepare yourself for the best possible outcome. Keep the positive attitude as you work through the challenges.

Keeping a notebook or even a piece of paper and pencil around is a great way to define what it is that you want. Writing it down makes it something you can focus on. Asking how you can attain it gives your imagination the opportunity to kick into action. Solving a problem or achieving the goal keeps you motivated to continue using your imagination to transform your life for the better.

# Chapter 24

## Get Out of Control

There are many things in your life that are within your control: when you wake up, when you go to sleep, and how you approach the different things that you need to do each day. What you decide to wear is in your control. How you respond to people's words or actions is within your control. However, there are also many things in your day that are not within your control. The weather. What other people say or do. What other people think of you. Many people get very attached to the idea that they should control as many things as they can. In fact, they are prepared to be very happy when they can control things and very unhappy when they cannot.

When you attach your frame of mind to things that you cannot control, it can be very challenging. When it's raining, you feel gloomy. When it's sunny, you feel cheerful. You let outside forces control your emotions. You allow your circumstances to decide how you will feel. So, if everyone around you acts the way you want them to, you are happy. If they don't act the way you want them to, you are unhappy. When everything goes your way, you are happy. When you don't get everything you want, you are unhappy. Often when you don't get what you want, you try to change the circumstances to get your way. This is a trap. You think that manipulating everything and everyone around you will bring you happiness, which is to say that if everything goes your way you will be happy. When it doesn't go your way, then you try to control more things so that you will be happy. The trap continues.

Here's the problem. You cannot control anything but yourself. You never could control anything but yourself, and you will never be able to control anything but yourself. If you try to control everything outside of yourself, you will never have everything you want. Your day will never be 100 percent of everything you want, how you want it, and when you want it. Trying to control everything outside of yourself because you think it will bring you happiness is not only frustrating, it's useless. The need to control everyone and everything will cause you to focus on all of the things that are not going your way.

The key to being happy is to let go of trying to control everything that is outside of you. Instead, spend your time focusing on what is going well for you right now. Be happy for those things. Also, understand that all the things that are going your way are temporary, so enjoy them while you can. When it seems like nothing is going your way, remember that this too is temporary.

Can you think of a time that you tried to control a situation or a person's actions? How did that make you feel?

_____

_____

_____

_____

_____

Describe a time that you felt angry or resentful because you didn't get what you wanted.

_____

_____

_____

_____

_____

How did you try to control that situation? Did you manipulate anyone in this process? (Remember that manipulating others is not a healthy way to grow your self-respect.)

_____

_____

_____

_____

_____

Make a list of things that you try to control.

_____
_____
_____
_____
_____
_____

Circle any of these things are completely within your control.

Write down as many things as you can think of that are going well in your life right now. Remember that being thankful for your good fortune attracts more positive things.

_____
_____
_____
_____
_____
_____
_____
_____
_____

Compare your thoughts and emotions about things you are trying to control with the thoughts and emotions about things that are going well in your life right now. Which list brings you more happiness?

___

___

___

___

___

___

___

# CHAPTER 25

# What if All of Your Misfortunes Were Your Fortunes?

There's an old story of a farmer. He had only one horse to help work his farm. One day the horse ran away. His neighbor said, "That's too bad." The farmer replied, "Maybe, maybe not." Two days later the horse returned and brought two other horses with him. Now the farmer had three horses. The neighbor said to the farmer, "This is great!" The farmer replied, "Maybe, maybe not." The farmer's son decided that he wanted to ride one of the horses. While riding the horse, he fell off and broke his leg. The neighbor said to the farmer, "That's terrible." The farmer shrugged his shoulders and said, "Maybe, maybe not." The following day men from the government came to the countryside and took all of the able-bodied young men to fight in the war. The farmer's son was spared because he had a broken leg. The point of the story is that the farmer realized that he couldn't control all the things that happened around him. He was also not attached to the idea that everything that happens is either good or bad. This story is an example of how misfortunes can become fortunes.

Here is an example that you might relate to more easily. You get in an argument with a friend. You say some things that aren't very nice and your friend says some things that aren't very nice. This is a misfortune. Or is it a fortune? Before you decide whether or not this is good or bad, let's examine this a little further. What did you say that wasn't very nice? What does that say about you as a person? Do you like what it says about you? What if you thought about it and decided that you didn't like what your actions said about you as a person? Perhaps that argument lets you reflect on yourself and become a better person. Fortune.

Now, what did your friend say to you in that argument? What does it tell you about that person? Does it tell you something that causes you to change your opinion of them? Does it tell you that they are truly a good person and they are deserving of your friendship? Or does it tell you that they are not someone that you should allow to influence your life? Was what they said truly unkind or was it coming from a place of hurt because you were unkind first?

The argument gives you an opportunity to make a choice. Do you apologize and start on a path to improve your own character? Do you learn about someone else's character and then find a new direction that leads you to people who are truly your friends? Every misfortune has a lesson to teach you. If you spend your time trying to decide if the experience is good or bad, you miss the opportunity to learn the lesson that the experience teaches you.

When you are faced with misfortune, have you ever said to yourself, "Why does this always happen to me?" The simple truth is that it keeps happening because the lesson will repeat itself until you learn it. When you keep getting in arguments with the same person, you are missing the lesson. If you want to improve your life, stop thinking that anything that happens to you is a misfortune. The effort you make in overcoming the challenges will make you stronger, smarter, and more confident.

Think of a time when something happened that you thought of as "bad." What was this event?

_____

_____

_____

Now, change your perspective. What positive outcomes were possible because of this thing that happened?

_____

_____

_____

_____

If you had seen this "bad" event as positive, how could that have changed what happened next?

_____

_____

_____

_____

_____

What would it feel like if you decided to find the best thing in every difficult situation?

___

___

___

___

___

If you decided to find something positive in every difficult situation, how would it change your reaction to the difficult situations that come your way?

___

___

___

___

___

# CHAPTER 26

# A Story of Two Monks

Here is a little story about two monks. A monk is defined as a member of a religious community of men typically living under vows of poverty, chastity, and obedience. They usually wear robes or simple clothes and shoes.

Two monks, Noah and Yesah were walking along a path until they came to the edge of a river. At the water's edge there was a woman kneeling on the ground and crying. Noah said to the woman, "What is troubling you?" The woman explained that when she left in the morning the river was very low and she was able to cross it easily. Now, she was returning home and the river was too high for her to cross. Her young child would miss her if she didn't get home and would certainly cry through the night if she did not return. Hearing her story, Noah agreed to help her across the river by carrying her safely to the other side. So, the three of them proceeded across the river and when they had reached the other side, Noah placed her on the ground and the woman continued on her way home to the west and the monks continued on their way to the east.

About a half hour later, Yesah, who was growing angrier and angrier, said to Noah, "Our master said we should never look at a woman; we should never speak to a woman; and we should never touch a woman. You have done all these things. You know, you have disobeyed our master." Noah looked at Yesah and replied, "I put that woman down a half an hour ago, yet you still carry her."

Grudges are ideas that we carry around with us. The longer you carry them, repeat them, and hold on to them, the more they weigh you down and the angrier you become. From Noah's perspective, he did the right thing. His beliefs allowed him to help another person and in turn help her small child. However, Yesah's perspective was that Noah should not have disobeyed their master. Which monk is correct?

**Finding Personal Success**

Often people hold grudges against other people for something that they said or did. If you examine the reason for holding that grudge it is usually because the person you are angry with did something in a specific situation that you would have done differently. If something happens and you have to make a decision that you feel is the best way to handle the situation, you make your choice and then move on. When someone else makes a decision that you don't agree with, you hold a grudge. From your perspective, they were wrong for doing what they did or saying what they said. In this moment you allow the decision of another person to weigh you down, bother you and cause you to have negative thoughts about them. They did not share your perspective about the situation.

Reflect on Chapter 24 about control. You hold that grudge because they didn't do what you would have done, which is another way of saying you wish you could control other people's words or actions.

There are times that grudges last for a few minutes or days to years and even decades of time. Family members can hold something against another family member because they would have done something differently. Over time these feelings can create a rift in a family, and people can go years without speaking to each other. Often this is a case of one person thinking they are right and trying to reverse time and control a situation that is already over. Instead, if you look at the other person's perspective or ask them why they chose to do what they did, there would be no reason for any anger or resentment.

Is there anyone you are holding a grudge toward right now? How recent was their action that you found offensive (hours, days, months, years)?

_____

_____

_____

_____

_____

Write down why you think their action was wrong.

_____

_____

_____

_____

_____

Now, from the other person's perspective, write down all of the possible reasons that they chose to do what they did.

___

Which of those reasons would explain their motivation for their actions?

___

If none of them seem reasonable, you may not share many common values with this person. Perhaps it is time to put down the grudge and take the weight off of yourself. Understand that you have a very different perspective and seek people who share your beliefs and values.

# Chapter 27

## Creating a Good Day

Complete these questions before you read any further.

1. Are you having a good day or a bad day?
2. Why are you having a good day or a bad day?

_____

_____

_____

3. What kind of day do you want to have tomorrow and the next day and the day after that?

_____

Look at your answers to these questions and focus on the second one. Whether or not you are having a good day or not is not as important as examining why you are having this kind of day. Let's say for argument's sake that you are having a good day. Why are you having a good day? If your day is going well because something or someone else made you feel happy, you need to examine the things that influence your feelings. If you are waiting to get something or have something else happen to be happy, you are outsourcing your happiness. Relying on someone else to make you happy is handing over the control to create your own mood and letting something else determine if you are going to have a good day.

Being happy is actually something that you are in complete control of because it happens in your mind. The three questions that you answered at the beginning of this chapter all exist in your mind. So too does your happiness or misery. When you let your outer circumstances determine your level of happiness, you have lost control of your reality.

Look back at your answer to the question, "Why are you having a good day or a bad day?"

4. How much of your happiness is attached to something that is out of your control?

___

5. How much of your happiness is attached to something that is within your control?

___

6. What would it take for you to reduce the things listed under the question #4, about how much of your happiness is out of your control?

___

7. How would focusing on the things within your control to create your happiness feel?

___

8. How would shifting your focus of where you find happiness affect your life?

___

9. Write down one or two things that you attach your happiness to. Then rethink these attachments and write down how you could feel happy regardless of these outside influences.

___

# CHAPTER 28

# Life is 10 Percent What Happens to You and 90 Percent How You React to It

Anyone who knows anything about the great American sport of football has certainly heard the name Tom Brady. Tom Brady is arguably one of the greatest NFL football quarterbacks in the history of the game. Having played in nine Superbowl games during his 18 years in the league is only one record that he holds. You might think that Tom was always a superstar. You might think that anyone with this kind of reputation on the football field must have natural ability. You would be wrong.

Tom Brady was picked number 199 out of 254 players in the NFL draft in 2000. Here are some excerpts from his scouting report for that draft:

- Poor build, skinny
- Lacks physical stature and strength
- Lacks mobility and ability to avoid the rush
- Lacks a really strong arm
- Can't drive the ball downfield
- Does not throw a really tight spiral
- System-type player who can get exposed in forced to ad lib
- Gets knocked down easily

In interviews, Tom Brady has often spoken about how he took this report and set his goals to work on everything that was on that list. He could have chosen a lot of different responses. Instead, he decided to listen to the football experts and improve his skills in the areas where he was lacking. Now, the rest is history.

You may not have an interest in football or have ever set foot on a football field, but the lesson here is about what you do with criticism. We get criticism from many places. Family, friends, teachers, coaches, bosses, and even strangers can all toss out less than flattering comments. The scouts that reviewed Tom Brady certainly didn't spare his feelings when they wrote their report. Their job is to identify which players a team would pick to make a winning team. They were not concerned with the player's self-esteem. They wanted their money's worth.

Take a moment to think about what you do with criticism. Do you get offended? Maybe you say things like, "Can you believe what she said?" or "That guy has a lot of nerve saying those things about me." People love to be offended. It gives them a feeling that in any particular circumstance they are in right and whoever made a critical remark is wrong. Let's face it, everybody likes to be right more than they like to have it pointed out that they are wrong. It's natural to get angry when someone criticizes you. However, once the emotion of anger passes it's a good idea to take an objective look at the criticism and learn from it.

Here are some tools to help you make the most out of criticism.

1. Decide if the criticism is accurate. Be honest with yourself. Do they have a reason to criticize you? If you examine the comment, and it isn't accurate, let it go. Let go of being offended and get on with your day. If it is accurate, then use the criticism to improve what you're doing.
2. Look at what you are doing or not doing from an objective perspective. From the perspective of the person criticizing you, is the comment aimed at improving you or demeaning you? If the comment was something that you need improvement on, use the information to work on yourself or a particular skill. If the comment was demeaning, let it go. If you have trouble seeing this from an outside perspective, ask a trusted friend or family member.
3. Use the criticism to your fullest advantage. Did your English teacher give you a C- and comment that you have a particular issue with grammar? Did your coach tell you that the reason you sit the bench is because you don't take practice seriously and are lackadaisical during skill drills? Does the band teacher give you something to work on because you aren't getting a particular music progression that you need for the upcoming concert? Take their criticism and work on it.
4. Ask for constructive criticism. Are you second string? Not in the select band ensemble? Having academic trouble? Getting a lot of criticism at home? Instead of grumbling and walking away or sulking as you warm the bench, ask the expert in charge what you should be doing to improve. They know and they will tell you, but they need to know that you want to get better at something.
5. Set a goal for yourself so you will know when you have used the criticism to your fullest advantage. I will have achieved my goal when…. I am playing on the first-string team, special chorus group, achieve a particular grade in a specific subject, or whatever you want to achieve. Use the critique to motivate you where you need to improve.

Think about a time that someone criticized you. How did you feel?

_____

_____

_____

How did you respond to the situation?

_____

_____

_____

If the criticism was accurate, did it motivate you to improve or discourage you? Did you use it to help you improve?

_____

_____

_____

_____

What would happen if you used criticism to reflect on yourself and improve in some way?

_____

_____

_____

_____

Who would you trust to ask for criticism about yourself?

_____

_____

_____

_____

# The Key to Success

Before you read any further, answer the following questions.

What do I want?

_____

Why do I want it?

_____

_____

How am I going to get it?

_____

_____

_____

A lot of people want things. Some want material things like expensive cars or clothes. Some want status such as to be the boss of a big company or to have high-ranking job. Still others want fame and the billboards and public recognition that comes with being high profile on TV, in sports, or in movies. There are people who want to be happy and enjoy the little joys in each day. These examples describe very different kinds of success.

However, the key to success is the same for everyone. Consistency. In order for you to have what you want it takes a consistent effort on your part. No one who owns their own company, stars in movies, or has earned a lot of money has done it all at once. They worked at it consistently. How did they get it? Well, they knew what they wanted. They knew why they wanted it. Finally, they figured out how they were going to get it. After that, they worked on it every day and took every opportunity that they got.

There are a lot of things that we do consistently. Imagine that in order to take care of your teeth, the only thing that you did was go to the dentist twice a year. Do you know what would happen to your teeth? They would fall out. The reason you still have your teeth is because you brush them every day, consistently. It's not a secret and most people want to keep their teeth which is why they take some time each day to take care of them.

How do you think athletes become world-class? Practice? Yes. Every day? Yes. Even when they don't feel like it? Yes. Movie stars have their own path. Casting calls and many rejections are not unfamiliar to famous people. They are so focused on their ambition to be an actor that they are willing to do any other job that they can get so they can keep searching out opportunities for fame. If you want to be the boss, that takes consistency too. Start at the beginning and learn everything you can. Move up the ranks until you are the boss. You can also learn from companies and then take what you learn to build your own business and be the boss. Either way, they work at it every day.

Look at what you wrote at the start of this chapter. What do you want? That's key to getting on the road to success. If you don't know where you're headed, you're probably not going to get there. Decide what is most important to you and use that to guide your choices.

Now, think about why you want this. This is your motivation. If your top motivation is to show off for your friends or to make somebody else happy, you are less likely to follow through on this goal. Motivation comes from having an internal desire to achieve something. Only when you are internally driven toward a goal will you work toward it with consistency.

Finally, how are you going to get it? The path you travel depends on what you want. It's different for everybody. So too is the path that leads many people to the same goal. Someone who wants to start a business might first work at a business and learn how it's done before they start their own business. Someone else might work for several businesses and get different styles of running a company. Another person might decide to create their own business from scratch and figure out the solution to each problem as it arises. In the end, each person can have their own business but how they got there can be very different. What do they all have in common? Consistency. They worked at it every day. They took their opportunities and used them to their advantage.

What are some things that you do every day consistently?

_____

_____

_____

Why are you doing these things?

___

___

___

___

Why is consistency important for these things?

___

___

___

___

What is something that you are not doing consistently that would help you get what you want?

___

___

___

___

How would doing this consistently affect the direction of your life?

___

___

___

___

___

# Chapter 30

## Get Your Hands Dirty

This book began with the topic of your dirty mind. Remember that your mind is like a pile of dirt. What you plant there will grow. Watch your thoughts. Now for the last exercise, it's time to get your hands dirty. Imagine that your life is a garden. Every positive thought that you think or kind act is a beautiful, healthy, and beneficial plant. It will grow in your garden and each time you think another positive thought or do another kind act, you will water and nurture that healthy garden. However, every negative thought that you think or unkind act is a weed. These weeds grow every time you think negative thoughts or carry out unkind acts toward yourself or others. If you are going to create a life that is filled with health and beauty, you need to start pulling out the weeds. And more importantly, you must stop planting more weeds. Those negative thoughts and actions are competing with your healthy thoughts and actions for water, sunlight and space to grow.

Think about the thoughts that you have planted in your mind. Now it's time to do some weeding.

1. Let go of the grudges that you hold against people and the anger or resentment you hang on to from past hurts. Some of these are small and you can easily forgive the person who hurt you. Some of them are bigger and will take some deep digging to get rid of. Get a shovel and start digging. Everyone has reasons for their actions, and we can't possibly understand the circumstances everyone else has to go through. Even if someone was mean to you, it may not have had anything to do with you. You might want to make a list of these grudges or things you are angry about and then just let them go one at a time. Start with the little things and it will make it easier to let go of the bigger ones.

2. Forgive yourself for the negative things you have said and done to others. Then, whenever possible, apologize to those people. This is hard work and pretty uncomfortable. However, this is the equivalent of pulling out the weeds and the rocks. It makes room for the healthier thoughts and actions to grow. This

is true especially if someone was mean to you as a response to something that you said or did. Apologize and do it sincerely.

3. Start planting positive thoughts and kind actions in your day. Start with some simple things. Put a note on your mirror that helps you start your day on a positive note. "Today, all things are possible." "Choose kindness," "I will only have this day one time, make it amazing," or anything that speaks to you. Make a tally on your notebook cover or a slip of paper in your pocket. Put a check mark every time you see someone being kind. Put a check mark every time you say or do something nice for someone. After a while you won't need a paper and check marks. You will have grown a habit and the positivity will water itself and continue to grow.

4. Take a few minutes each day to sit and calm your mind. Close your eyes and focus on the flow of your breath. Slow down the train of thoughts that constantly bombards your mind. It's almost impossible to stop all the thoughts, but take a few minutes to slow them down can be a great way to get rid of any ideas that you keep repeating to yourself that are not helpful. This is also a good way to solve problems. Ask yourself for the solution to a problem that you have or a question that you want to answer. As you slow down your thoughts, the solution often appears. Once you open your eyes, notice your breath. Try to maintain that state of mind as you go through your day.

5. At the end of the day, before you go to bed, write down at least three things that you are grateful for from your day. You can keep it in a journal, a notebook, a pad of paper or whatever is comfortable. Just write it down. Creating an awareness of kindness and gratitude in your life will water and shine like the sun on your garden of thoughts. This practice will brighten every part of your life.

Once you have a beautiful and healthy garden growing, you will find that positivity will be attracted to you. Negative people and their unkind acts will not affect you in the same way they did before. They will have to go somewhere else to plant their weeds and toss their rocks. You will find positive people and see acts of kindness.

The title of this chapter is "Get Your Hands Dirty." Recognize that having a happier life takes some effort. Things like attitude, gratitude, and consistency make the difference between achieving what you want and waiting around for something good to happen. You are in control of many of your choices. You can choose your response to every situation. What you decide to do when you are frustrated, angry, unhappy, or criticized makes the difference in how you feel about yourself. Ultimately, how you feel about yourself drives the choices that create your life. Choose wisely.

Use the pages that follow to help you work through the five activities listed above. Because these activities can be repeated again and again, consider designating a notebook or journal to continue writing down your thoughts and observations.

Keep this book. It is filled with ideas and information about yourself that was relevant at this time in your life. However, if you go back and reread any chapter three months or a year from now you will likely have very different answers. It is reusable and applies to your life exactly as it is at any point in time. Ultimately, becoming aware of your thoughts, goals, actions and choices is the act of a mature adult. You're on your way! I wish you enormous success. How you define that is entirely your choice.

For more inspiring questions and ideas, you can also follow me on Instagram @thepowerofchoiceforsuccess. I'd love to see you there!

Please let me know if you found this book helpful by leaving a review on Amazon, messaging me on Instagram @thepowerofchoiceforsuccess or emailing me at the thepowerofchoiceforsuccess@gmail.com. I'd love to hear what you have to say and you will be helping me create my next book and additional content for teens. Finally, if you have a friend that you think would like this book, please let them know. Thank you for choosing to go on this personal journey. I wish you the greatest success.

www.ingramcontent.com/pod-product-compliance
Lightning Source LLC
LaVergne TN
LVHW061333060426
835512LV00017B/2671